FATHER BENEDICT

JAMES F. DAY

FATHER
BENEDICT

THE SPIRITUAL AND INTELLECTUAL
LEGACY OF POPE BENEDICT XVI

SOPHIA INSTITUTE PRESS
Manchester, New Hampshire

Sophia Institute Press
Box 5284, Manchester, NH 03108
1-800-888-9344

www.SophiaInstitute.com

Sophia Institute Press® is a registered trademark of Sophia Institute.

Library of Congress Cataloging-in-Publication Data

Names: Day, James F., author.
Title: Father Benedict : the spiritual and intellectual legacy of Pope
    Benedict XVI / James F. Day.
Description: Manchester, New Hampshire : Sophia Institute Press, 2016. |
    Includes bibliographical references.
Identifiers: LCCN 2016025141 | ISBN 9781622823376 (pbk. : alk. paper)
Subjects: LCSH: Benedict XVI, Pope, 1927-
Classification: LCC BX1378.6 .D39 2016 | DDC 282.092—dc23 LC record
available at https://lccn.loc.gov/2016025141

First printing

For the faculty, administrators,
staff, and students,
past, present, and future, of
St. Michael School, Independence, Ohio

CONTENTS

FATHER BENEDICT

INTRODUCTION

At Mass on March 25, 2012, at Bicentenario Park in Léon, Mexico, only a few knew that the celebrant was suffering from a contusion on his head, concealed by the white papal zucchetto. He would complete the voyage, including a visit to Cuba, but it would prove to be the 265th Bishop of Rome's final trans-Atlantic journey. Exactly a year later, Jorge Bergoglio, as Pope Francis, would embark on his first Holy Week liturgical events, with images of his Holy Thursday service at the Prison for Minors in Rome seizing the world.

The night before, while staying at the house of the Capuchin Sisters in Léon, Pope Benedict XVI, struggling to find his way around the dark, unfamiliar room, slammed his head, causing a bleeding wound.

That night in Mexico, his head bleeding, a month shy of eighty-five, and having steered the barque of Peter for seven years under a hostile antipathy toward the Church, a drained Benedict XVI knew that his last gift to give would possibly be his greatest — and most unexpected. Just as no Jesuit becomes pope, no pope leaves the office alive. Yet both things happened in 2013.

Not since Gregory XII in 1415 had the supreme pontiff of the Roman Catholic Church resigned — a resignation that ended the Schism (1378–1417) that had spawned numerous antipopes. Before Gregory, Pope Celestine V abdicated in 1294 and was canonized less than twenty years later. In light of Benedict's announcement on February 11, 2013, his April 2009 visit to L'Aquila, torn apart by an earthquake three weeks earlier, took on new significance: during that visit, Benedict laid his pallium on the tomb of Saint Celestine V at Santa Maria di Collemaggio. The significance of this gesture should not undermine the Pope's presence that day to express solidarity with those whose lives were disrupted and lost by that earthquake. "The stop in the Basilica of Collemaggio to venerate the remains of Pope Saint Celestine V gave me an opportunity to feel tangibly this city's wounded heart," he said to the crowd gathered in L'Aquila. "My homage is intended as a homage to the history and faith of your region and to all of you who identify with this Saint."

As symbolic as that image might seem in hindsight, Benedict was not the only successor of Saint Peter to pray before the memorial to the medieval pope who resigned. Both Paul VI, in 1966, and Pius XII, in 1948, visited Celestine's tomb. Paul VI seriously contemplated resignation and seclusion to Monte Cassino, the monastery built by Saint Benedict in 529. It was a notion that many successors of St. Celestine have contemplated but never attempted—until Joseph Ratzinger.

It was in Monte Cassino in 2000 that, secluded from the modern world for a few days, German publicist Peter Seewald interviewed Cardinal Ratzinger on Catholic theology—an interview that would later be published as *God and the World: Believing and Living in Our Time*. This was not their first collaboration. A few years earlier, *Salt of the Earth* became a spiritual smash hit, revealing that the prefect of the Congregation for the Doctrine of the Faith was not a remote authoritarian figure disconnected from the trials of life. He was a pastor very much aware of the modern travails of the spiritual journey. The partnership would continue through Benedict's pontificate with *Light of the World* in 2010, highlighting Pope Ratzinger's prescient views as well as his accessibility to the average reader. These works from Peter Seewald invite us to spend time with the man Joseph Ratzinger, refreshingly candid as he ruminates spontaneously on the contemporary socio-religious landscape. More impressive than his own perspective is the recurring commentary on the reconciliation between the believer and the world, and of a healthy balance between faith and reason.

> Being Christian must not become a sort of archaic stratum to which I cling somehow and on which I live to a certain extent *alongside* of modernity. Christianity is itself something living, something modern, which thoroughly shapes and forms all of my modernity—and in this sense actually embraces it.

"God is the real central theme of my endeavors," Joseph Ratzinger confesses. Through dozens of published books, lectures, articles, retreats, letters, homilies, and interviews over six decades, his spirituality emerges, the soul of a true priest exposed. As one journeys with him, the theologian gives way to the spiritual sage: he really believes in what he says. His spiritual mentor, the Italian-born German priest Romano Guardini, wrote of his own book *The Conversion of Augustine*, "The present work on Augustine does not attempt to add anything to the body of historical research on the man. Its only aim is to present his personality and thought in the everlasting form of his writings as a perennial possibility of Christian existence." The same is attempted here about Joseph Ratzinger.

Ratzinger served as cardinal-prefect of the Congregation for the Doctrine of the Faith for almost a quarter of a century. The role of the office—the former holy office of the Inquisition, the dogmatic strong arm for the Pope—and the perception of its German enforcer earned him some clever nicknames: *panzerkardinal,* God's Rottweiler, German Shepherd. And even if his ascension in 2005 as Benedict XVI infused a renewed pastoral vitality and spirit within him, the more commanding public perception remained, casting Joseph Ratzinger as the cold, doctrinal authoritarian.

By the end of his pontificate, this popular view toward him persisted and he remained overall unfavorable, even as a steady undercurrent of devotion quietly developed. At this time, two monstrous crises were unfolding. Within the Church festered the earthshaking sexual-abuse crisis. Outside the Church, the dissolution of ethical standards that characterized the rise of rampant secularism. To Benedict, the suspension of objective truth—the abandonment of divine love—was the root of them both. Nevertheless, Benedict alone seemed accused of being the root of the abuse problem. But still he forged on, becoming the first pope to meet, repeatedly, with victims of clergy sexual abuse.

With Benedict's character under fire—that he was ill equipped to lead, that his life's trajectory did little for the concerns of the day—it seemed that the media construction of him would prove too well fortified to debunk. But, on the contrary, his life had prepared him precisely for the age of the millennium. He had survived under Nazi rule. He was a firsthand observer of and contributor to the Second Vatican Council. He was a university professor in a country split between contrasting ideologies, with Soviet communism and Western democracy each tugging at the reforming German heart—a heart that beat most passionately in the universities where he lived and worked. Decades later his students continued to meet — often with Ratzinger present — indicating the enduring influence of the professor-theologian. He could both grasp and articulate the malaise and acedia of peoples while offering hope for their redemption. Yet, in spite of all these things, he was made the prime target in a culture crying for tolerance even as anti-Catholicism remained the last acceptable prejudice. "Anyone who is not aware of the intellectual caliber of Benedict simply reveals his own incompetence or incomprehension," James V. Schall, S.J., wrote shortly after Benedict's abdication.

"The person who thinks the Pope only concentrates on books, far away from people's real problems," Benedict's secretary of state, Tarcisio Cardinal Bertone, said in 2012, "is very mistaken." Whenever he was called in for a new role of service, Benedict inevitably redoubled his efforts with urgent news to share. In responding to the era of unbelief, he renewed his own vocational commitment. And fearlessly, as a Pope in his seventies and eighties with nothing to lose, he treaded unguarded and open before peoples in ways no politician could ever dare. He challenged nations on their own turf, whether in Paris, London, or Berlin — asserting with compassion and conviction that God could not be excluded from the public square while reminding the faithful that victory had been won on the Cross. Man's mortal self, however, suffers from an "epidemic of heart," he said after his retirement, which "leads to corruption and other dirty things, those that lead man only to think of himself and not of the good."

In spite of observations of a world gone awry, Benedict's testimony to living a joy-filled life rooted in the triune God and to the Holy Spirit's presence as an active, living force shone forth in his pontificate. "Where joylessness rules and humor dies, we may be certain that the Holy Spirit, the Spirit of Jesus Christ, is not present."

And because the resignation of Benedict XVI has often been spun as a narrative of weak leadership forced out by corrupting agendas around him, it may be easy to forget that it occurred during the Church's Year of Faith, convoked by Benedict to run from October 2012 to November 2013. That such a theme was integral to the Pope's agenda for fostering a sense of critical awareness that the gift of faith could no longer be taken for granted in the public sphere was demonstrated in the document Benedict wrote announcing his intention for the Year of Faith, *Porta Fidei* (The Gate of Faith): "Ever since the start of my ministry as Successor of Peter, I have spoken of the need to rediscover the journey of faith so as to shed ever clearer light on the joy and renewed enthusiasm of the encounter with Christ."

It often happens that Christians are more concerned for the social, cultural and political consequences of their commitment, continuing to think of the faith as a self-evident presupposition for life in society. In reality, not only can this presupposition no longer be taken for granted, but it is often openly denied. Whereas in the past it was possible to recognize a unitary cultural matrix, broadly accepted in its appeal to the content of the faith and the values inspired by it, today this no longer seems to be the case in large swathes of society, because of a profound crisis of faith that has affected many people.

A profound crisis of faith that has affected many people: this is what concerned Joseph Ratzinger throughout his life. This is what he sought to cure in those disillusioned by material accumulation and constant distraction, burdened by stress and unhappiness—that they might be reintroduced to the Source of life, to find mystery in a time of predictability. Benedict XVI, in the mold of the great popes throughout history, stood as a warrior of faith, encouraging those who dared to listen and spurred on by their own conversions to follow his lead into their own Westminster Halls and Reichstags, their own Areopagi. Fond of citing Augustine, Benedict clearly saw that what was being played out at this very time mirrored Augustine's observation of the battle between the "city of the flesh" and the "city of the spirit." This was the quintessential "Christian situation, this battle between two kinds of love."

"But in the end, it can only be a proposal," Monsignor Lorenzo Albacete once said of faith. "The greatness and mystery is our freedom. We can accept it. We can move on to something else." The only proposal worth dying for, as put forth by Benedict XVI, is to seek out Christ, and He has given us a lifetime of signposts to follow in every aspect of life: in formation of the Christian faith, in loving others, in personal vocation, in education, and in how we see the surface of the natural world and the beauty around it. It means not blind obedience but an embrace of one of Benedict's favorite themes: the freedom and the will of the human person to respond accordingly to that proposal. Our reluctance to do so in this day and age may echo Franz Kafka's warning to his friend: "Christ is an abyss of light, into which, unless you close your eyes you will fall headlong." Beauty, Pope Benedict believed, is what is revealed once we have overcome fear.

Through his lifetime of bridge building, Benedict XVI proposes to be the Virgil to the Dantes of our generation, calling for both a New Evangelization and a new metanoia—a sacramental return to Christ and His Church. The Father of the West who guided the poet has become the Holy Father who did the un-thinkable, and now wishes simply to be called Father Benedict.

CHAPTER ONE

THE PROPER STUDY
OF MANKIND

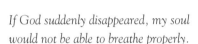

If God suddenly disappeared, my soul
would not be able to breathe properly.

—Peter Seewald, *Benedict XVI: An Intimate Portrait*

George Weigel's book *The End and the Beginning*[1] describes metanoia as a conversion so significant as to form a new life. Benedict XVI epitomized this metanoia in his vocation as priest and
particularly in his relinquishment of the role of "servant of the
servants of God." Having seen firsthand the wrenching, public
way of the cross lived out by Pope John Paul II, only to be chosen as his immediate successor to shepherd a wounded Church,
Benedict knew that with his own increasing frailty he would not
re-create for the faithful what John Paul II displayed. But that
did not mean he would not experience his own passion.

---

[1] George Weigel, *The End and the Beginning: Pope John Paul II:
The Victory of Freedom, the Last Years, the Legacy* (New York:
Doubleday, 2010).

Weigel describes "affective conversion" as "emptying ourselves of dehumanizing passions and ordering our emotional lives and our imaginations toward the truly good and beautiful, who is God." While writing of John Paul II, Weigel may well be referencing the Polish Pope's close confidant and successor, Benedict XVI:

> The paradox of metanoia, which was manifest in the life of Karol Wojtyła, is that all this emptying of self leads to the richest imaginable human experience: a life unembittered by irony or stultified by boredom, a life of both serenity and adventure.

"From early on," Ratzinger confided to Peter Seewald, "I had to communicate. I could not help but share with others what I had learned." Two addresses in the months leading up to his resignation in February 2013 give us a sense of Pope Benedict's state of mind. Knowing that the pending announcement would shake the already tenuous foundations of the Church, communicating the joy of the gospel was still the message he sought to share. On his eighty-fifth birthday in April 2012, Benedict remained hopeful in the radiant love of Christ:

> I am now facing the last chapter of my life and I do not know what awaits me. However, I do know that the light of God exists, that He is Risen, that His light is stronger than any darkness, that the goodness of God is stronger than any evil in this world.

Just three months before proclaiming to the world that "due to advanced age" he would be resigning the papacy, Benedict visited the Community of Sant'Egidio's home for the elderly, Viva gli Anziani, "as an old man visiting his peers." He said, "When life becomes frail, in the years of old age, it never loses its value and its dignity: each one of us, at any stage of life, is wanted and loved by God, each one is important and necessary."

When Joseph Cardinal Ratzinger dreamed of retiring from his post as prefect of the Congregation for the Doctrine of the Faith — John Paul II refused his resignation three times — he envisioned returning to Bavaria to live with his elder brother, Fr. Georg, or remaining inside the Vatican writing in the library. That dream evaporated when the College of Cardinals selected him to guide the Church in 2005. For Benedict XVI, it was just another call to obedience. Almost eight years later, on the eve of what would alter the course for the faithful as well as his own life, he said at the Sunday Angelus: "The human person is not the author of his own vocation but responds to the divine call. We must rely more and more on the power of his mercy, which transforms and renews."

Noting that the following day, the memorial of Our Lady of Lourdes, was the World Day of the Sick, he added, "With prayer and affection I shall be close to all the sick." The next morning, in a brief speech delivered in Latin before the assembled cardinals, Benedict XVI confirmed that on that World Day of the Sick he would be the one finally to accept his own resignation.

"In order to govern the barque of Saint Peter and proclaim the Gospel, both strength of mind and body are necessary, strength which in the last few months has deteriorated in me to the extent that I have had to recognize my incapacity to adequately fulfill the ministry entrusted to me," he bluntly stated. In the flood of media attention that ensued, the decision of the increasingly fragile Bishop of Rome, whose service was often dismissed, lampooned, and rejected, was seen as a graceful act of humility and dignity, noble and brave—and not the least bit expected. It was also an action that paved the way for the emergence of a global phenomenon.

"Anyone carried home by the people today, may be condemned tomorrow," Sydney Carton warns in the Dickens classic *A Tale of Two Cities*. Jorge Bergoglio's arrival as Pope Francis in 2013 and his quick embrace by those otherwise disinterested in the Church came at a price: a negative, often vindictive attitude toward Benedict. The invitation to joy that motivated the Benedictine papacy, and even the modesty and grace of his stepping down, did not alter the premature obituaries. Pope Benedict's launching of the Year of Faith in October 2012 that took him to Lebanon, Mexico, and Cuba and even the publication of his final volume of *Jesus of Nazareth* seemed to have little effect on the public at large.

In 2011, actress Susan Sarandon referred to Pope Benedict as "this Nazi one we have now." Other than cries from the Catholic League, she suffered no significant backlash. A statement from the Anti-Defamation League calling on her to apologize for her "attack on the good name of Benedict XVI" concluded: "Ms. Sarandon may have her differences with the Catholic Church, but that is no excuse for throwing around Nazi analogies. Such words are hateful, vindictive and only serve to diminish the true history and meaning of the Holocaust."

If segments of the public longed for a revolution within the Vatican after Benedict XVI's departure, they got it. Yet quite simply and practically, there would likely be no Francis without Benedict. Even to suggest such an idea, however, provokes disbelief and scorn. For as radical as Pope Francis's papacy has been viewed in uprooting standard Vatican protocol, it was Benedict's resignation that opened the door to the Francis era. Benedict's retirement left several officials perturbed, and several possible reasons for his retirement—including scandal, conspiracy, and health—were quick to surface. Who was prepared for such an unorthodox move from such an orthodox pope? The obituary that so many had prematurely prepared would now have to be rewritten. The assessment of his legacy had to be delayed and his contribution to culture reevaluated. But for the true believer, the secular unpopularity of Benedict XVI was an indication of his success as Pontiff: Christ was also unwelcomed by keepers of the status quo (cf. Luke 4:24).

A growing number of those who recognize Benedict's lifetime contribution to the Church and to the world continue to stoke the flame in the face of public opinion, among them J. Steven Brown, editor of the Benedict XVI compendium *A Reason Open to God.* "His contribution will take the Church hundreds of years to sort out," Brown attests. Commentaries relating the former theology professor's thoughts over the years to the roots of today's tumultuous global events continue to emerge, including Benedict's prophetic thoughts on Islam, faith, and reason in light of ISIS's horrific executions. And while he has kept his promise to devote his remaining years to prayer and remain hidden from the public, rare words from the retired Benedict XVI have emerged to encourage his listeners quietly, such as in his message to Urbaniana University in 2014: "Whoever has experienced great joy cannot keep it simply for himself. He must pass it on to others."

"Jesus *must* offend us," Peter Kreeft writes in *Back to Virtue,* "for he tells us not what we want to hear but what we need to hear, and sin has inserted a great gap between our needs and our wants." Overcoming the shifting winds of thought so as not to lose sight of God gradually became Joseph Ratzinger's vocation within a vocation. He came to recognize that all pervading ideologies that are counter to Christianity ultimately fall into the dominating force of moral relativism. The slogan of this movement that seeks to usurp God and His Church is perhaps best described by the eighteenth-century English poet Alexander Pope in his poem "An Essay on Man": "The proper study of Mankind is Man." In his 1907 apocalyptic novel *Lord of the World*, Monsignor Robert Hugh Benson expresses this ideological shift: "God, as far as He could be known, was man."

"We have a different goal: the Son of God, true man. He is the measure of true humanism," Cardinal Ratzinger stated in his homily just before the cardinals entered the Sistine Chapel for the 2005 conclave. This assertion, so simple as to go unnoticed even among believers, is that great stake that the humanistic ideology espoused by relativism seeks to uproot. We see opposition to it throughout Sacred Scripture, beginning with the serpent's hiss in Genesis: "You shall be as gods," and in Jesus' life and in His parables, especially that of the tenants in the vineyard (Matt. 21:33–44).

Pope Benedict devoted a significant portion of his book *Jesus of Nazareth: From the Baptism in the Jordan to the Transfiguration* to the parable of the tenants — the parable wherein the owner of the vineyard sends his son to obtain the produce from the tenants only to be killed. Not only was the parable an evocative reference to Jesus' impending death, but the Pope extends its relevance to today's vineyard tenants. "Isn't this precisely the logic of the modern age, of our age?" he asks. "Let us declare that God is dead, then we ourselves will be God." He continues:

At last we no longer belong to anyone else; rather, we are simply the owners of ourselves and of the world. At last we can do what we please. We get rid of God; there is no measuring rod above us; we ourselves are our only measure. The "vineyard" belongs to us. What happens to man and the world next? We are already beginning to see it.

The proper study of mankind is God, and the beauty of the vineyard shall be preserved. Knowing this, Joseph Ratzinger can confidently extend the invitation to "seek that which is above" (Col. 3:1). In one of his catecheses on prayer, Pope Benedict did not encourage "contempt of earthly realities" but asserted that we "must live in this world, in the heart of the earthly city, as new men and women." This involves seeking the things that are above, namely, "compassion, kindness, lowliness, meekness, and patience.... And above all these things put on love, which binds everything together in perfect harmony" (Col. 3:12, 14).

To love genuinely and authentically necessarily involves the presence of God, and this is what Benedict reminded us as his urgent first message: God is love. This is the logical longing of human thought, and by its illumination it exposes the recoiling lies of relativism as it closes in on itself, cowering from the eternal abyss of Light, as Kafka warned.

"My grace is sufficient for you, for power is made perfect in weakness," the Lord says (2 Cor. 12:9). Vulnerability, humility, dignity, grace, and loyalty: we see these traits in Pope Benedict in his unprecedented resignation and in his "wish to also devotedly serve the Holy Church of God in the future through a life dedicated to prayer," as he said in his "Declaratio" on February 11, 2013.

The remarkable transition to the pontificate of Pope Francis, for all of the change he brought, was seamless—even when current pope meets retired pope, which Francis continues to do before every international trip. "It's like having your grandfather in the house, a wise grandfather" is how Pope Francis described the presence of the emeritus bishop of Rome.

"It is beautiful to be old!" exclaimed Benedict to his peers at the Sant'Egidio elderly home. "We must never let ourselves be imprisoned by sorrow!... In our faces may there always be the joy of feeling loved by God and not sadness." That Benedict continued to promote the youthful joy of living as a child of God into old age in both word and action, amid surrounding temptations to despair, testifies to his vocational fidelity and to the veracity of his message.

The same year as his appointment as archbishop of Munich and Freising, 1977, Professor Father Joseph Ratzinger, at age fifty, published *Eschatology: Death and Eternal Life*, his theological study on the last things—namely, death, judgment, heaven, and hell. He does not water down the subject matter or offer his thoughts as abstract ruminations; instead he reflects on how the last things are meant to influence living day by day. A passage on suffering indicates his sense that even in the 1970s the meaning of suffering had little place in the new world order.

"The attempt to do away with suffering through medicine, psychology, education and the building of a new society has grown into a gigantic bid for the definitive redemption of mankind," he writes. "Of course, suffering can and should be reduced by these means. But the will to do away with it completely would mean a ban on love and therewith the abolition of man."

Eschatology shows the subject of death, already then on Joseph Ratzinger's mind, as it pertains to man's overall destiny. "If we do not accept and respect death," he said in 1985, "we do not accept and respect life either." More than thirty years after the publication of *Eschatology*, Pope Benedict XVI spoke further on the topic in a candid dialogue with Salesian Father Pietro Riggi at a meeting with clergy from the Diocese of Rome. Father Riggi referenced a previous comment Benedict made about "how seldom 'the last things' are mentioned today" and asked for elaboration.

Benedict, launching into a five-paragraph, off-the-cuff response, acknowledged the rare appearance of the themes of the last things in modern Catholic thought. "I think we have all been struck by the Marxist objection that Christians have only spoken of the afterlife and have ignored the earth. Thus, we demonstrate that we are truly committed to our earth and are not people who talk about distant realities," he said.

But he reaffirms the need to look honestly at the last things in order to help the earth and man's place in it. He continues:

> When one does not know the judgment of God one does not know the possibility of Hell, of the radical and definitive failure of life, one does not know the possibility of and need for purification. Man then fails to work well for the earth because he ultimately loses his criteria, he no longer knows himself—through not knowing God—and destroys the earth. All the great ideologies have promised: we will take things in hand, we will no longer neglect the earth, we will create a new, just, correct and brotherly world. But they destroyed the world instead.

Time and again Joseph Ratzinger emphasizes that when God is declared dead, the substitutes for God, which are called by various names, are ultimately the same and lead to the same destructive behavior. As he has set out to show us, the only real alternative to these human idols is the one that has withstood every attempt to smother it. "Somewhere deep down," he said, "man knows: I have to be challenged, and I have to learn to form myself according to a higher standard." That higher standard informed every aspect of his life, even when domineering events threatened time and again to seize the vineyard of its true tenant once and for all.

CHAPTER TWO

THE PROPHET
FROM BAVARIA

———————— ✵ ————————

Vatican City, April 2005

In April 2005, the dean of the College of Cardinals, the cardinal-prefect Joseph Ratzinger, guided the interregnum period in which the Chair of Peter sat vacant after the death of John Paul II—leaving an impression on not a few observers. He was consistently a voice of steadiness and comfort during a time of strongly visceral emotions. He also celebrated his seventy-eighth birthday and was eager to complete his responsibilities and finally retire in peace.

And so, in his homily at the Mass before one of the most anticipated conclaves in Church history, Cardinal Ratzinger did not mince words. He also coined a defining phrase. For anyone who felt the world shifting increasingly beyond recognition, the "dictatorship of relativism" succinctly identified the dominant ideology of the time.[2] Because Ratzinger had addressed this

---

[2] For a comprehensive study of Joseph Ratzinger's stratagems against relativism, see Gediminas T. Jankunas, *The Dictatorship*

theme as far back as thirty-five years earlier, Peter Seewald, in his biographical work, *An Intimate Portrait*, believed that the homily to the cardinals "was in some sense a concentration of the fruit of all his research and thinking."[3]

Citing a passage from Ephesians, the second reading of the liturgy: "so that we may no longer be infants, tossed by waves and swept along by every wind of teaching arising from human trickery," Cardinal Ratzinger segued into the now-famous part of the sermon:

> How many winds of doctrine we have known in recent decades, how many ideological currents, how many ways of thinking? The small boat of thought of many Christians has often been tossed about by these waves, thrown from one extreme to the other: from Marxism to liberalism, even to libertinism; from collectivism to radical individualism; from atheism to a vague religious mysticism; from agnosticism to syncretism; and so forth. Every day new sects spring up, and what Saint Paul says about human deception and the trickery that strives to entice people into error (cf. Eph. 4:14) comes true.
>
> Today, having a clear faith based on the Creed of the Church is often labeled as fundamentalism. Whereas relativism, that is, letting oneself be "tossed here and there, carried about by every wind of doctrine", seems the only attitude that can cope with modern times. We are moving toward a dictatorship of relativism, which does not

---

of Relativism: Pope Benedict XVI's Response (Staten Island: Alba House, 2011).

[3] Seewald, *An Intimate Portrait*, 35.

recognize anything as certain and which has as its highest goal one's own ego and one's own desires.

And yet, while it is generally perceived that this relativism, this great cultural and moral danger facing the Church, is largely an outside force, Ratzinger was here describing the thought and manner of the Roman Catholic Church in 2005. "*We* are moving towards a dictatorship of relativism."

Who else would hold up the uncomfortable mirror? With the Church's reputation in shambles, tarnished by scandal within the Vatican, one is reminded of the words of Jesus: "You hypocrite, first take the log out of your own eye, and then you will see clearly to take the speck out of your brother's eye" (Matt. 7:5). The cardinal said so himself: "Many no longer believe that what is at issue is a reality willed by the Lord himself."[4]

A month before the conclave, a fed-up Cardinal Ratzinger stepped in for a dying John Paul II to preside over the annual *Via Crucis*, the Way of the Cross ceremony at the Colosseum on Good Friday night. The meditation for the ninth station was a harsh indictment of the cloud of relativism seeping into the Church:

> How often do we celebrate only ourselves, without even realizing that he is there! How often is his Word twisted and misused! What little faith is present behind so many theories, so many empty words! How much filth there is in the Church, and even among those who, in the priest-hood, ought to belong entirely to him! How much pride, how much self-complacency!

---

[4] Ratzinger with Messori, *Ratzinger Report*, 45.

All of the meditations for the Stations of the Cross that year can be read in relation to a Church that had deserted the very God who founded her. And all were written by Joseph Cardinal Ratzinger.[5]

Although exposing the dictatorship of relativism was a commitment over decades, it was not until the events surrounding the death of Pope John Paul II that opportunities emerged for Ratzinger to address it on such a scope. To avoid doing so would betray his great love for the God and the Church he served his whole life.

Bavaria, 1927–1951

Joseph Ratzinger was raised in Bavaria, the youngest of three children. Both his father, a policeman, and his mother were people of faith. Through his parents the future cardinal and pope experienced the aura of the Roman liturgy, of centering everything on God. "I know of no more convincing proof for the faith than precisely the pure and unalloyed humanity that the faith allowed to mature in my parents and in so many other persons I have had the privilege to encounter," he reflects.[6]

Joseph was five when Hitler was appointed chancellor of Germany in 1933. On his fourteenth birthday he was conscripted into the Hitler Youth, much to his and his family's chagrin — his father was an adamant opponent of the Nazis, which got him into trouble every so often. Ratzinger chronicles his involvement as a teenage would-be soldier. He deserted the German army as Allied

---

[5] Joseph Ratzinger, "Way of the Cross at the Colosseum," March 25, 2005.

[6] Joseph Ratzinger, *Milestones: Memoirs, 1927–1977* (San Francisco: Ignatius Press, 1998), 131.

forces gained ground and the end became clearly imminent. He and others were rounded up by American troops and placed in a German POW camp, although Ratzinger seems to take pains to downplay the drama of the episode. He paints an evocative picture of the impending fall of the Nazi regime while undergoing military training in 1944. His superiors were "fanatical ideologues who tyrannized us without respite." He illustrates the image of a spade, an instrument of labor with profound meaning:

> We were trained according to a ritual invented in the 1930s, which was adapted from a kind of "cult of the spade", that is, a cult of work as redemptive power. An intricate military drill taught us how to lay down the spade solemnly, how to pick it up and swing it over the shoulder. The cleaning of the spade, which was not to show a single speck of dust, was among the essential elements of this pseudo-liturgy.... Now the rituals with the spade came to an end, and every day we had to ride out to erect tank blockades and trenches.... When we came home exhausted in the evening, the spades, which previously could not have a single speck of dust, now hung from the wall full of big clods of clay; but no one cared. Precisely this fall of the spade from cultic object to banal tool for everyday use allowed us to perceive the deeper collapse taking place there. A full-scale liturgy and the world behind it were being unmasked as a lie.[7]

When the war ended, Joseph was released from the POW camp and returned to his pursuit that the war temporarily interrupted, studying for the priesthood. He and his older brother,

---

[7] Ibid., 33–34.

Georg, were ordained on the same day, June 29, 1951, the feast of Saints Peter and Paul.[8]

It was the Catholic Faith that nurtured Joseph's perseverance during the reign of Nazi terror. His Catholic Faith was indeed what had been left standing amid the broken dreams of the SS. That same Faith was the sole anchor for a seminarian in Poland named Karol Wojtyła, the future Pope Saint John Paul II. And it was waiting for both of them in what would become a lifelong relationship with that Church. In the face of domineering totalitarianism, or, as Ratzinger puts it, "the destruction ideology of the brown rulers; in the inferno that had swallowed up the powerful," the Church nevertheless "stood firm with a force coming to her from eternity. It had been demonstrated: the gates of hell will not overpower her."[9] For if the Nazi regime embodied pure hell, the witness of those whose deaths testified to God's standard showed "that the house built on rock had stood firm."[10] And so, sixty years later, as a septuagenarian priest, the young man who had emerged from the Nazi conflagration walked through the gates of Auschwitz as Pope Benedict XVI, determined to lead the push against today's armies of evil: "Let us cry out to God, with all our hearts, at the present hour, when new misfortunes befall us: whether it is the abuse of God's name as a means of justifying senseless violence against innocent persons, or the cynicism which refuses to acknowledge God and ridicules faith in him."[11]

---

[8] Georg Ratzinger as told to Michael Hesemann, *My Brother, The Pope* (San Francisco: Ignatius Press, 2011) contains fascinating accounts of the war period.

[9] Ratzinger, *Milestones*, 42.

[10] Ibid.

[11] Benedict XVI, address during visit to the Auschwitz Camp, May 28, 2006.

Liturgy, sacraments, family: these were where faith was best expressed for Joseph Ratzinger. His description in *Milestones* of the death of his father, who had seen his sons mature into young priests and glimpsed Joseph's burgeoning theological talents as a rising professor, conveyed the warmth of his familial foundation: "We were grateful that we were all able to stand around his bed and again show him our love, which he accepted with gratitude even though he could no longer speak."[12] Yet, although a Christian's hope lies in "the life of the world to come," grief is no less potent. "When I returned to Bonn after this experience," he continues in detailing the loss of his father, "I sensed that the world was emptier for me and that a portion of my home had been transferred to the other world."[13]

Milestones ends when Ratzinger is appointed archbishop of Munich-Freising. He expresses that each calling to a position of greater responsibility took him a step further from fulfilling what he really wanted to do: write books on theology. Yet Ratzinger never desired the "prestige" of being archbishop, prefect, or pope. He was a priest in the truest sense of the word, what Peter Seewald called "a servant of truth."[14] "Here was someone for whom God's irruption into the world through Jesus Christ is an absolute reality," Seewald writes.[15]

1968

With his theological studies complete, Joseph Ratzinger became a peritus under Cardinal Frings of Cologne at the Second Vatican

---

[12] Ratzinger, *Milestones*, 119.
[13] Ibid.
[14] Peter Seewald, ed., *Pope Benedict XVI: Servant of Truth* (San Francisco: Ignatius Press, 2006).
[15] Seewald, *An Intimate Portrait*, 224.

Council and later took a position at the University of Tübingen, recruited by the dean of Catholic theology, Hans Küng. There Ratzinger observed the initial years of the implementation of the Council. And there he personally witnessed the tumult of the 1968 student revolutions within his own university and ministry. The perfect storm had arrived. Much ink has been spilled over an ideological shift in Joseph Ratzinger's theology as a result of that turbulent time—typically billed, in political terminology, as a swing from progressive to conservative thinking.[16] It was in this season of tumult that Ratzinger would write and publish *Introduction to Christianity*, based on a series of university lectures he had delivered. It appealed not only to the learned—Cardinal Wojtyła, for one, eagerly consumed it in the Soviet-shrouded Eastern bloc—but also to the everyday seeker of truth. As the title of its first chapter, "Belief in the World Today," indicates, the theologian reveals an inherent understanding of the struggle of assenting to something outside oneself. This pastoral approach at the book's outset invites the reader to a metanoia, a turning from the visible alone to the transcendent. "Man's natural inclination draws him to the visible," he writes. "He must turn around to recognize how blind he is if he trusts only what he sees with his eyes. Indeed belief *is* the conversion in which man discovers that he is following an illusion if he devotes himself only to the tangible."[17]

Introduction to Christianity is a surprisingly accessible companion for meditation on the great mysteries of faith—perhaps

---

[16] John Allen, Jr., *The Rise of Benedict XVI* (New York: Doubleday, 2005), 150–152.

[17] Joseph Ratzinger, *Introduction to Christianity* (San Francisco: Ignatius Press, 2004), 51.

the greatest gift of the Bavarian priest as a theologian for the nonstudent. Amid so much skepticism even within circles of theologians and believers, the book unabashedly addresses criticisms, unbelief, and doubt, but always emerges promoting the Faith in the Person of Christ: "Such faith is not the acceptance of a system but the acceptance of this person who is his word; of the word as person and of the person as Word."[18]

Ratzinger realized that one could no longer take the tenets of faith for granted. Amid the societal chaos around him, the time had come for the mild-mannered theologian to set out in service of Christ as John the Baptist did. He surely knew that he would face hatred and scorn, that he would be labeled, and that by his countercultural stance, millions of ears would be closed to his insights. "This is where the present book comes in," he writes in the preface to the original 1968 edition of his *Introduction to Christianity*. "Its aim is to help understand faith afresh as something that makes possible true humanity in the world of today."[19]

The book's very existence proved to be a beacon for the truths of the Faith during a time of vocal and physical assault on such claims. There were even rumors, possibly perpetuated by Hans Küng, that students attempted to seize Professor Ratzinger's microphone and eggs were hurled at him in the packed lecture halls of Tübingen as a symbol of mutiny.[20] Nevertheless, Joseph Ratzinger's lectures were a must-see at the university at a time when "German-speaking professors of theology had become rock stars."[21] The desire for clarity in a time of tumult was palpable.

[18] Ibid., 205.
[19] Ibid., 32.
[20] Seewald, *An Intimate Portrait*, 89.
[21] Anthony Grafton, "Rereading Ratzinger: Pope Benedict XVI, the Theologian," *New Yorker*, July 25, 2005, 44.

During his papacy, Benedict's penetrating insights tempered a similar moral confusion. Seewald noted that to Ratzinger, a new era had dawned in the post–Vatican II period: "He had seen how crucifixes were removed from schools under the Third Reich, but now it was precisely theologians who, in leaflets and graffiti, were mocking the crucified Christ as a sadomasochist."[22]

Do not forget what we believe, Joseph Ratzinger steadily taught amid the upheavals in *Introduction to Christianity*. And if you do doubt, *etsi Deus daretur*, "believe as if God existed." "He takes nothing from you," the newly installed Benedict XVI said at his inaugural Mass, "and he gives you everything."[23] Ratzinger used the Creed as the structure of *Introduction to Christianity*. Even in 1968, troubled by the developments within and outside the Church, Joseph Ratzinger noticed that the *Credo*, beginning with "I believe in one God," was losing its practical meaning as the true song of revolution in the everyday life of the Catholic believer.

Why I Am Still in the Church—Ratzinger in the 1970s

The acceleration of secular modernity's separation from faith and reason—combined with the Church's postconciliar growing pains—lay at the heart of the tension. Prayer and the sacraments were no longer the believer's driving force, now having to compete with the immediate gratification offered through advanced technology. The notion of salvation was being replaced with the "quality of life." Thomas E. Woods aptly conveyed this attitude: "The religious convictions of a people have in our day

---

[22] Seewald, *An Intimate Portrait*, 90.
[23] Benedict XVI, homily, April 24, 2005.

become like museum pieces, interesting curiosities to an unbelieving world."[24]

Two works in the immediate period after the publication of *Introduction to Christianity* indicate quite clearly that one could no longer take for granted basic truths of the Faith that had been largely unquestioned for centuries. The first work emerged as a series of radio addresses that Professor Ratzinger, employed at the University of Regensburg, delivered in 1969 and 1970. A few months later, in June 1970, the professor delivered a lecture in Munich entitled "Why I Am Still in the Church Today" to an audience of almost a thousand. Both display Joseph Ratzinger, now in his early forties, as simply unleashed.

These pieces were later published in the book *Faith and the Future*. A passage from it hints at a coming winter of discontent:

> From today's crisis will emerge a church that has lost a great deal. It will no longer have use of the structures it built in its years of prosperity. The reduction in the number of faithful will lead to it losing an important part of its social privileges. It will become small and will have to start pretty much all over again. It will be a more spiritual church, and will not claim a political mandate flirting with the Right one-minute and the Left the next. It will be poor and will become the Church of the destitute.[25]

---

[24] Thomas E. Woods Jr., *How the Catholic Church Built Western Civilization* (Washington, DC: Regnery Publishing, 2005), 224.

[25] Joseph Ratzinger, "What Will the Church Look Like?," in *Faith and the Future* (San Francisco: Ignatius Press, 2009), 116. See also Marco Bardazzi, "Ratzinger's forgotten prophecy on the future of the Church," Vatican Insider, February 18, 2013, accessed August 26, 2015, http://vaticaninsider.lastampa.it/eng/.

The language, evoking the desires later vocalized by Pope Francis ("I want the Church to go out to the street!"), suggests that a few years after Vatican II, Ratzinger was seeing that believers no longer functioned in an accepting, positive society in which one's life was centered in a vibrant parish community. An old era had indeed passed. It had become, to quote the original title of fellow Bavarian Werner Herzog's 1974 film *The Engima of Kaspar Hauser*, a time of "Every Man for Himself and God against All."

Indeed, a real crisis of faith, belief, and truth—simply, relativism—not only had spread over Western culture but had infiltrated the Western Church. Thus, it was only a matter of time before Joseph Ratzinger had to confront this real crisis directly. By 1970, the immediate exuberance after Vatican II had slowed; the reality of how thunderous the change had been and the difficulty in dialogue with the modern world was beginning to strain.[26]

In response, Ratzinger saw an authentic communion of faith as the only viable solution. "I remain in the Church because I view the faith—which can be practiced only in her and ultimately not against her—as a necessity for man, indeed for the world, which lives on that faith even when it does not share it."[27] Here, in 1970, he already foresaw modernity's endgame: to achieve the age of man. "For if there is no more God—and a silent God is no God—then there is no longer any truth that is

---

[26] See Dietrich von Hildebrand, *Trojan Horse in the City of God* (Manchester, NH: Sophia Institute Press, 1999).

[27] Joseph Ratzinger, "Why I Am Still in the Church Today," in *Fundamental Speeches from Five Decades*, ed. Florian Schuller (San Francisco: Ignatius Press, 2012), 149.

accessible to the world and to man."[28] He knew a new dictatorship was unfolding, not of a political regime but of the heart, trading real freedom for a false freedom: "In a world without truth, however, one cannot keep on living." Yet in his continual joy and hope, he suspects that hearts still recognize that truth cannot be abandoned: "Even if we suppose that we can do without truth, we still feed on the quiet hope that it has not really disappeared, just as the light of the sun came to an end, momentarily disguising the worldwide night that had started."[29]

Bridge Building in the Digital Age

In a 1973 sermon revised into part of the book *The God of Jesus Christ*, Professor Ratzinger hints at how far humanity as consumer might go when the inevitable digital revolution arrives. It is a key understanding in the Bavarian prophet's belief that isolating faith from reason would lead not to greater enlightenment or freedom but to societal harm. It also reveals a prescient understanding that the fomentation of the dictatorship of relativism is marked by technological transformation.

"The Revelation of John speaks of the adversary of God, the 'beast,'" he begins. "This beast, the power opposed to God, has no name, but a number. The seer tells us: 'Its number is six hundred and sixty-six' (13:18). It is a number, and it makes men numbers."[30] Relativism's reduction of people to numbers, commodities, statistics, and data returns later as a theme in Benedict XVI's first encyclical, *Deus Caritas Est*. "We who lived through

---

[28] Ibid.
[29] Ibid.
[30] Joseph Ratzinger, "God Has Names," in *The God of Jesus Christ: Meditations on the Triune God* (San Francisco: Ignatius Press, 2002), 23.

the world of the concentration camps know what that means," he continues.

> The terror of that world is rooted in the fact that it obliterates men's faces. It obliterates their history. It makes man a number, an exchangeable cog in one big machine. He is his function—nothing more. For when functions are all that exist, man, too, is nothing more than a function. The machines that he himself has constructed now impose their own law on him: he must be made readable for the computer, and this can be achieved only when he is translated into numbers. Everything else in man becomes irrelevant.…
>
> Whatever is not a function is—nothing. The beast is a number, and it makes men numbers. But God has a name, and God calls us by our name. He is a Person, and he seeks the person. He has a face, and he seeks our face. He has a heart, and he seeks our heart. For him, we are not some function in a "world machinery". On the contrary, it is precisely those who have no function that are his own.[31]

Even in the 1970s Ratzinger recognized that the total embrace of the digital behemoth would inevitably usurp the pursuit of truth. How could one argue the existence of objective truth when he could construct an entire reality—an entire truth—in the digital realm? What use is there for the God as taught by a faith, let alone an ancient faith? "Today, many people can hardly understand any more that behind a human reality stands the mysterious divine reality."[32]

---

[31] Ibid.
[32] Ratzinger with Messori, *Ratzinger Report*, 157.

Here Joseph Ratzinger, even if reluctant to assume the mantle following John Paul II, served as a bridge builder just when the explosion of instantaneous images reached unmatched heights. It was left to him to man the ship while ideologies pressured the Church to conform, and while scientific, political, and pragmatic principles became increasingly indifferent to the standard of Western thought, creativity, beauty, and hope. The greatest victims of this climate were the youth. Joseph Ratzinger addressed his concern and hope for their spiritual renewal during World Youth Days in Cologne, Sydney, and Madrid. This concern is captured in the 2000 preface to his classic *Introduction to Christianity*:

> The dismal and destructive ecstasy of drugs, of hammering rhythms, noise, and drunkenness is confronted with a bright ecstasy of light, of joyful encounter in God's sunshine. Let it not be said that this is only a momentary thing. Often it is so, no doubt. But it can also be a moment that brings about a lasting change and begins a journey.[33]

If anyone within the Church could lead a response to the events of the third millennium, it was he. Benedict XVI embodied what a *Pontiff* truly is, from the Latin word for "bridge builder." Building bridges does not come without peril, betrayal, and the Cross. That Benedict sensed this is evident in his first papal homily, when he pleaded for the faithful's prayers: "Pray for me, that I may not flee for fear of the wolves." With grace and fortitude, the prophet from Bavaria forged into the deep. His encouraging words and examples as a priest show us the way, for this

---

[33] Ratzinger, *Introduction to Christianity*, 19.

current revolution is far from its completion, and more voices are needed. What lies at stake is nothing less than the eradication of the truths espoused by the oldest existing institution.

CHAPTER THREE

STRIKING AT THE ROOT OF SIN

The sole moral value that exists is the future society in which everything that does not exist now will be fulfilled.

—Joseph Ratzinger, *A Turning Point for Europe?*

Joseph Ratzinger strove to embody the passage he frequently cited: "[I]t is no longer I who live, but Christ who lives in me" (Gal. 2:20). Embodying this passage requires an authenticity in living the Christian Faith, an articulation of its beliefs, and a readiness "to make a defense to any one who calls you to account for the hope that is in you" (1 Pet. 3:15). But it will likely make you unpopular.

The pursuit of truth took Pope Benedict into areas in which truth was blanketed. Sometimes he would venture into the political arena or into cultures in which basic rights recognized

This chapter has been expanded from my article, "Benedict XVI and the Roots of Injustice," *Crisis Magazine*, May 20, 2015, http://www.crisismagazine.com/.

in the Catholic Faith were muddled or absent. "The crisis of faith that is increasingly making itself felt by Christian people is revealing itself with increasing clarity as a crisis regarding awareness of fundamental values of human life," he wrote in 1975.

Henry David Thoreau reflected, "There are a thousand hacking at the branches of evil to one who is striking at the root." One hundred thirty years later, Joseph Cardinal Ratzinger told Vittorio Messori: "Those who really desire a more human society need to begin with the root, not with the trunk and branches, of the tree of injustice." Here Ratzinger referred to unjust social and economic structures and said that "personal sin is in reality at the root" of them. But mankind, the cardinal seems to indicate, looks elsewhere for solutions rather than dealing with the heart of the matter. If personal sin is the root of unjust structures and everything prejudiced, these evils can be displaced only by destroying the sin through the effort of turning toward God. Yet for many people today who are comfortable in our "sinless" world, conversion to God may not be an appealing step toward enlightenment.

A year after the end of World War II, Pope Pius XII remarked, "Perhaps the greatest sin in the world today is that men have begun to lose the sense of sin." This statement indicates the growing awareness of a separation between God and man. The defeated powers of World War II displayed a violent and atheistic mindset and were intent on liquidating anybody who shared different beliefs. Since then, the attempt to rid culture of Christianity has unraveled in subtler forms. In the third millennium, for instance, we see a more "humanistic" approach, one that strives for unity without a God. This was not lost on Cardinal Ratzinger:

> The danger of a dictatorship of opinion is growing, and anyone who doesn't share the prevailing opinion is

excluded, so that even good people no longer dare to stand by [such] nonconformists. Any future anti-Christian dictatorship would probably be much more subtle than anything we have known until now. It will appear to be friendly to religion, but on the condition that its own models of behavior and thinking not be called into question.

Throughout his life and work, Joseph Ratzinger has been convinced that personal sin is indeed the source of man's pervading unhappiness and alienation from others and from God. Therefore, change can come only by recognizing where sin festers in the world and by recognizing our need for God in uprooting it. The problem is not simply man's fallen nature but a rampant "apatheism"—the opinion that it makes no difference whether God exists. This ideology is imposed by a pop culture that has superseded diverse cultures and the religions associated with them. It has replaced mystery with the tangible.

Relativism is thus the only acceptable path by which man can avoid accusations of bigotry or offensiveness and threats to personal freedoms. "What is left, if skepticism and relativism—despite all their partial usefulness—are not, on the whole, a path?" asked Ratzinger. "Are we not directed anew to man's self-transcendence, to the path of faith in the living God?"

To the growing dictatorship of personal opinion, Christianity had become one of the many thousands of opinions. Some consider it a hypocrisy, marred by its own shortcomings and public perception. But in boldly addressing the challenges of relativism during his pontificate, Benedict exposed the roots of the tree of injustice and offered the authentic alternative proposed by the Faith. He showed that Church teachings are for the betterment of mankind and offer an illuminating spiritual pathway to the divine, in spite of misapprehension, preconceived notions, and critiques that such teachings are outdated and irrelevant. The truth, Benedict XVI has said again and again, truly does "make you free" (John 8:32).

The Banalization of Sexuality

During an interview on a flight to Cameroon in March 2009, Philippe Visseyrias asked Pope Benedict to respond to the claim that "the position of the Catholic Church on the way to fight [AIDS] is often considered unrealistic and ineffective." The Pope's answer became the most publicized aspect of the trip, with such headlines as "Pope's Anti-Condom Message Is Sabotage in Fight against AIDS."[34] A 2010 *Charlie Hebdo* magazine cover depicted Pope Benedict raising a condom in place of a Host, the blurb reading "*Ceci est mon corps*" — "This is my body."

"At this point, I really felt that I was being provoked, because the Church does more than anyone else," a riled Benedict declared in *Light of the World*. "The sheer fixation on the condom," he continued, "implies a banalization of sexuality, which, after all, is precisely the dangerous source of the attitude of no longer seeing sexuality as the expression of love, but only a sort of drug that people administer to themselves."[35] In spite of Benedict's answer that "condoms alone do not resolve the question itself," the media, in the Pope's own words, "completely ignored the rest of the trip in Africa on account of a single statement." This

---

[34] Ben Goldacre, "Pope's Anti-Condom Message Is Sabotage in Fight against AIDS," *Guardian*, September 11, 2010, accessed August 27, 2015, http://www.theguardian.com/.

[35] Benedict XVI and Seewald, *Light of the World*, 104.

included his homily at Ahmadou Ahidjo Stadium of Yaoundé, which supported the Church's position in aiding the physical plight of the African people while reaffirming spiritual truths:

> The first priority will consist in restoring a sense of the acceptance of life as a gift from God. According to both Sacred Scripture and the wisest traditions of your continent, the arrival of a child is always a gift, a blessing from God. Today it is high time to place greater emphasis on this: every human being, every tiny human person, however weak, is created "in the image and likeness of God" (Gen 1:27). Every person must live! Death must not prevail over life! Death will never have the last word![36]

Reporting of such rhetoric seldom raises a publication's circulation. Emphasizing contraception as a solution to a crisis implies a lack of understanding of the essence of human sexuality and an unwillingness to seek a solution based on responsibility, education, prevention, assistance, and, above all, truth. Venturing so far into the world of control and manipulation has resulted in a blurring of the true meaning of how and why life should enter the world.[37] Like a true pastor, Pope Benedict is very much concerned for a soul's conversion, for each person to allow himself to discover his name in the Creator's handwriting. A year before the 2009 Cameroon trip, in an address regarding marriage and the family, Benedict said, "The 'No' which the Church pronounces

---

[36] Benedict XVI, Homily during the Eucharistic celebration on the occasion of the publication of the *Instrumentum Laboris*, March 19, 2009.

[37] James V. Schall offers a prescient depiction of similar future events as early as 1971 in *Human Dignity and Human Numbers* (Staten Island: Alba House, 1971).

in her moral directives on which public opinion sometimes unilaterally focuses, is in fact a great 'Yes' to the dignity of the human person, to human life and the person's capacity to love."[38] Despite the veracity of this position toward an authentic way of life, mankind has created such a maze in its promotion of sexual liberties that truth, ethics, and responsibility are no longer issues. "The morality that the Church teaches is not some special burden for Christians," Cardinal Ratzinger wrote in 1988. "It is the defense of man against the attempt to abolish him. If morality—as we have seen—is not the enslavement of man but his liberation, then the Christian faith is the advance post of human freedom."[39]

Joseph Ratzinger remembered a noticeable culture shift in 1968, which began a new era. That spring, student revolutions shook Europe, while assassinations and riots battered the morale of the United States. That summer Pope Paul VI released his final encyclical, *Humanae Vitae* (*Of Human Life*), which reconfirmed Church teaching on human reproduction. "Rarely has a text in the recent history of the Magisterium become such a sign of contradiction as this Encyclical which Paul VI wrote after making an anguishing decision," Ratzinger observed.[40]

Humanae Vitae, according to D. Vincent Twomey in *Pope Benedict XVI: The Conscience of Our Age*, "almost split the Church in two." Twomey notes that the social revolutions of

[38] Joseph Ratzinger, "To Participants in an International Congress Organized by the John Paul II Institute for Studies on Marriage and the Family," April 5, 2008.

[39] Ratzinger, "Faith's Answers to the Crisis of Values," *Turning Point*, 44.

[40] Giovanni Maria Vian, "Humanae Vitae Marks 40," *L'Osservatore Romano*, July 1, 2008, 1.

that year "quickly degenerated into terrorism, a phenomenon that Joseph Ratzinger would later diagnose as a symptom of an underlying illness in society, an illness whose roots were intellectual and ultimately theological."[41]

It would be something he would continue to address as pope.

The Word and Reason

On September 12, 2006, a day after the fifth anniversary of the attacks on the United States that commenced the War on Terror, Benedict XVI spoke again at the University of Regensburg. His speech became the topic of controversy in the Muslim world and brought threats against him, condemnation from the West, and admonishments from French president Jacques Chirac: "We must avoid everything that increases tensions between peoples or religions."[42] The near-four-thousand-word address, "Faith, Reason and the University: Memories and Reflections," focused on the necessity of employing reason when it comes to contemplating God. But what sparked the controversy was a quotation that Benedict used "as the starting-point for my reflections."

Benedict considered the quotation, from the fourteenth-century Byzantine emperor Manuel II, to be "of startling brusqueness, a brusqueness that we find unacceptable." Yet it was immediately taken out of context by the press, resulting in explosive dispute. Manuel II had said, "Show me just what Mohammed brought that was new, and there you will find things only evil and inhuman, such as his command to spread by the sword the faith

---

41 Vincent Twomey, *Benedict XVI: The Conscience of Our Age* (San Francisco: Ignatius Press, 2007), 19.

42 Sam Coates and Deborah Haynes, "Al-Qaeda Threatens Jihad over Pope's Remarks," *Times*, September 17, 2006.

he preached." Benedict immediately followed with his point in quoting it: "The decisive statement in this argument against violent conversion is this: not to act in accordance with reason is contrary to God's law."[43]

Was Regensburg a grave blunder? As time wore on, Regensburg remained an infamous misstep in the pontificate in the mainstream eye. But writers and scholars took more and more note of it, particularly in light of subsequent violent events around the world. After the kidnapping and death of journalist James Foley at the hands of ISIS in August 2014, the themes of Regensburg resurfaced. Fr. George Rutler wrote, "[Benedict] condemned no one, and spoke only for truth without which the votaries of unreason, for whom there is no moral structure other than the willfulness of amorality, and whose God is not bound by his own word, rain down with destruction."[44] Rutler, like Ratzinger, suggests that such exposing of the roots of injustice will continue to be misinterpreted if we focus only on the branches and the tree itself.

Regensburg once again came to light in January 2015, after two young men stormed the *Charlie Hebdo* offices in Paris and gunned down the editor and ten associates. The attack was apparently a jihadist retort to a recent issue of the magazine featuring the prophet Mohammed on the cover and was quickly condemned across the West. A worldwide display of solidarity followed, with the viral taglines *#JeSuisCharlie* and "We are all *Charlie Hebdo*" and an estimated 3.7 million gathering for rallies

---

[43] Benedict XVI, lecture during meeting with representatives of science, September 12, 2006.

[44] George W. Rutler, "Benedict XVI: Pope as Prophet," *Crisis Magazine*, August 14, 2014, http://www.crisismagazine.com/.

a few days after the shooting. At the core of the public response was the defense of "freedom of expression," which celebrities, American politicians, and the French president François Hollande, among others, vigorously defended.[45] It's unclear when the popular *#JeSuisCharlie* hashtag stopped trending; actor Jared Leto received respectable applause for mentioning it at the January Golden Globes, but he left it out when presenting the Best Supporting Actress Oscar a month later. And so deeper issues remained, and few seemed willing to address the root causes—notably, limits to freedom of expression.

Sacred images are forbidden in Islam. The depiction of the prophet was considered an inappropriate portrayal (and not the first from *Charlie Hebdo*) and evidently drove the assailants to the fatal response. Pope Francis, two weeks after the attacks, would note in his in-flight interview following his Philippines voyage the necessity for prudence. He said:

> I cannot constantly insult, provoke a person continuously, because I risk making him angry, and I risk receiving an unjust reaction, one that is not just. But that's human. For this reason I say that freedom of expression must take into account the human reality and for this reason it must be prudent.[46]

A number of commentators picked up on the theme of judiciousness with regard to free speech. For Samuel Gregg, research

---

[45] Laurie Hanna et al., "We Are Here to Support Freedom. We Will Not Be Beaten," *DailyMail.com*, January 11, 2015, http://www.dailymail.co.uk/.

[46] Francis, in-flight press conference from the Philippines to Rome, January 19, 2015.

director at the Acton Institute, a terror attack such as the one on *Charlie Hebdo* can be understood only from a theological standpoint—something Benedict foresaw at Regensburg. "Many professional interfaith dialoguers didn't like the Regensburg address because it highlighted just how much of their discussion was utterly peripheral to the main game and consisted in many instances of happy talk that avoided any serious conversation about the real differences that exist between many religions," Gregg remarked shortly after the jihadist attack in Paris. "It also annoyed those who believe that all religions are ultimately the same and of equal worth."[47] George Weigel, less than two weeks after the assault, observed that now it is truly time to face the facts about where we are—and who we are—in both Europe and the world:

> In the world of *Charlie Hebdo*, sadly, all religious convictions (indeed all serious conversations about moral truth) are, by definition, fanaticism—and thus susceptible to the mockery of the "enlightened." But the crude caricature of religious belief and moral conviction is false; it's adolescent, if not downright childish; it inevitably leads itself to the kind of vulgarity that intends to wound, not amuse; and over the long haul, it's as corrosive of the foundations of a decent society as the demented rage of the jihadists who murdered members of *Charlie Hebdo*'s staff.[48]

---

[47] Kathryn Jean Lopez, "Rereading Regensburg," *National Review Online*, January 17, 2015, accessed August 27, 2015, http://www.nationalreview.com/.

[48] George Weigel, "Europe and Nothingness," *First Things*, January 20, 2015, accessed August 27, 2015, http://www.firstthings.com/.

Relativism — "The Most Profound Difficulty of Our Age"[49]

"The man of today will for the most part scarcely respond with an abrupt 'No' to a particular religion's claim to be true; he will simply relativize that claim by saying 'There are many religions,'" writes Cardinal Ratzinger in *Truth and Tolerance*.[50] Some intend the total eradication of religion. In the wake of the Paris shooting, the American Humanist Association, a nonprofit atheist group, sent out a viral post reading, "Religion isn't and shouldn't be protected from criticism. Those who break the law to enforce religious codes must be brought to justice. Freedom of speech, thought, and expression will never be destroyed. #JeSuisCharlie #Charlie Hebdo #Humanism."

Joseph Ratzinger has witnessed this recurring theme: to create a truly humane existence, tolerance and dialogue are only stepping-stones to a better world of authentic love and respect. Even those elements ultimately fall short: tolerance implies "putting up with" the other rather than genuine discovery; dialogue as an element of diplomacy is often successful only for its own sake rather than an inspiration to a real connection.

The tendency to consider anything religious to be irrelevant in the public square thus leaves a secular culture struggling to respond effectively to the likes of a *Hebdo* attack or to the ongoing assaults of ISIS. Samuel Gregg, George Weigel, and other observers cite Regensburg as one of the most important speeches of the twenty-first century. Islamic expert Samir Khalil Samir, S.J., claims that freedom of expression extends even to the Pope: "The aim of the Regensburg speech is precisely humanistic dialogue,

---

[49] Joseph Ratzinger, *Truth and Tolerance: Christian Belief and World Religions* (San Francisco: Ignatius Press, 2004), 72.

[50] Ibid., 23.

which rejects nothing positive in Islam or in the Enlightenment, but criticizes what is extremist or anti-spiritual in one and the other."[51]

Ratzinger's concern that ignorance about a culture leads to insensitivity, violence, and a vicious circle is due in large part to the current state in which Western culture has found itself. *Truth and Tolerance* argues that individual cultures are no longer able to make room for belief in the invisible, particularly in Christianity, because they must integrate themselves within the secular culture and its lifestyle. "We should not forget that Christianity, as early as the period of the New Testament, carries within itself the fruit of a whole history of cultural development." Ratzinger cites Egyptian, Hittite, Sumerian, Babylonian, Persian, and Greek culture. "All these cultures were at the same time religions, all-embracing historical ways of life." To relegate Christianity to something that is private and walled off from everyday life is to deny not only its relevance but its very reality. "The people of God is not just a single cultural entity," he continues, "but is gathered together from all peoples, therefore the first cultural identity . . . must always be struggling against the opposing weight of shutting off, of isolation and refusal."[52]

Christianity, then, is the conduit between a wholly secular worldview and an absolute transcendent perspective. "Faith and reason are like two wings on which the human spirit rises to the contemplation of truth," opens Pope Saint John Paul II's

---

[51] Samir Khalil Samir, S.J., "Church-Islam Dialogue: The Path Starts from Regensburg's Pope," AsiaNews, January 16, 2007, accessed August 27, 2015, http://www.asianews.it/.

[52] Ratzinger, *Truth and Tolerance*, 70–71.

encyclical *Fides et Ratio* (*Faith and Reason*), a text that bears a heavy Ratzingerian influence, "and God has placed in the human heart a desire to know the truth—in a word, to know himself—so that, by knowing and loving God, men and women may also come to the fullness of truth about themselves."[53] Through faith and reason we can know God and can understand ourselves and our reception of Him. In *Truth and Tolerance*, Ratzinger admonishes societies who decide that God is not relevant: "No one can understand the world at all, no one can live his life rightly, so long as the question about the Divinity remains unanswered. Indeed, the very heart of the great cultures is that they interpret the world by setting in order their relationship to the Divinity."[54]

Conversion from sin leads to a clear-eyed view of the fundamental nature of man, something we no longer quite grasp. Recall Pius XII's declaration that the greatest sin of the last century was a loss of the sense of sin. The root of the tree of injustice that Ratzinger mentions in *The Ratzinger Report* is nurtured by a relativistic acknowledgment of cultures that flattens diversity and heritage in the name of acceptance and equality. It tries to cultivate a goodness without God, a humanism without humanity, under the cover that truth cannot be known. This leads only to a false enlightenment, a "darkening of truth. This distorts our action and sets us against one another, because we bear our own evil within ourselves, are alienated from ourselves, cut off from the ground of our being, from God."[55] We have lost our own narrative as a people.

---

[53] John Paul II, *Fides et Ratio*, September 14, 1998.
[54] Ratzinger, *Truth and Tolerance*, 61.
[55] Ibid., 66.

With Great Joy

In Saint Luke's account of the first Christmas, the angel exclaims to the shepherds, "I bring you tidings of great joy" (2:10). That elated tone is also conveyed at the announcement of a new pope. After we see the white smoke and hear the bells of Saint Peter's, the cardinal-protodeacon appears on the loggia of the basilica to announce: *Annuntio vobis gaudium magnum habemus papam!* (I announce to you with great joy that we have a pope!)[56]

It is precisely under the banner of joy that Joseph Ratzinger has set us—a people in need of rediscovering its roots—on the path of the Good Shepherd. "Do not become discouraged in the face of difficulties and doubts; trust in God and follow Jesus faithfully and you will be witnesses of the joy that flows from intimate union with him," he once encouraged.[57]

While the media and their followers spoke of an "aging pontiff" and an "out-of-touch church," Joseph Ratzinger was busy fostering an altogether different perspective. To associate *joy* with him is to understand its true meaning and to recognize that preconceived notions of someone can be transformed after witnessing the person's authentic expression. For Benedict XVI, proclamation of the gospel is alive only if it is suffused with joy, as personified by his immediate predecessor and his successor. Benedict, less visibly but no less genuinely, clutched joy even amid

[56] The cardinal-protodeacon charged with proclaiming Joseph Ratzinger's election in 2005, Jorge Medina Estévez, milked the drama of the moment with particular relish. "Fumata blanca y anuncio elección Benedicto XVI," YouTube video, 52:35–54:57, posted by "carlos91391," March 11, 2013, https://www.youtube.com/watch?v=AmIVhAbOaZs.

[57] Benedict XVI, message for the 46th World Day of Prayer for Vocations, May 3, 2009.

Vatican rumormongering and as nearly insurmountable fatigue weakened him. "Joy is at the heart of the Christian experience," he wrote to the young in 2012 in a message that contained the word "joy" more than 115 times.[58]

Monsignor Joseph Murphy authored the book *Christ, Our Joy: The Theological Vision of Pope Benedict XVI* precisely because he saw joy as a central theme in the life and pontificate of Joseph Ratzinger. In an interview about his book, Monsignor Murphy wrote:

> An important question, which the Pope addresses in his writings, is whether there can be joy in the face of suffering and death. A merely superficial joy cannot withstand these difficult realities, which bring us face to face with the fragility of our lives and the question of ultimate meaning. However, Christian joy is something much more profound. It springs from knowing that the God of love is close to us in all the circumstances of our lives and, as the saints teach us, it is this that enables us to face illness, suffering and death with serenity, confidence and hope.[59]

And yet we forget that we live in the light of Resurrection faith, depicted at the end of Luke's Gospel with Jesus "lifting up his hands" and blessing the apostles (Luke 24:50). This is the image that Benedict chooses to conclude *Jesus of Nazareth: Holy Week*:

---

[58] Benedict XVI, message for the 27th World Youth Day 2012, March 15, 2012.

[59] Joseph Murphy, *Christ, Our Joy: The Theological Vision of Pope Benedict XVI* (San Francisco: Ignatius Press, 2008), 184.

The gesture of hands outstretched in blessing expresses Jesus' continuing relationship to his disciples, to the world. In departing, he comes to us, in order to raise us up above ourselves and to open up the world to God. That is why the disciples could return home from Bethany rejoicing. In faith we know that Jesus holds his hands stretched out in blessing over us. That is the lasting motive of Christian joy.[60]

---

[60] Benedict XVI, *Jesus of Nazareth: Holy Week: From the Entrance into Jerusalem to the Resurrection* (San Francisco: Ignatius Press, 2011), 293.

CHAPTER FOUR

A MARIAN WAY
OF BEAUTY

---※---

It would seem unlikely that the bookish Benedict XVI would have anything of value to share with more than two hundred artists when he met with them in the Sistine Chapel. His predecessor, as a young man, seriously contemplated a life on the stage and wrote his own plays and poems. Pope John Paul II's 1999 "Letter to Artists" remains a touchstone for a Catholic artistic revival. But the Bavarian theologian seemed out of his league when it came to the artistic expression. What could he convey to an international coterie of musicians, architects, actors, and other representatives of the arts? And how could it possibly be relevant to their visions and creations?

Joseph Ratzinger's personal encounter with the riches of art emerged primarily through music, specifically the piano. Later, as Pope Emeritus, when he accepted two honorary doctorates from Polish music academies, he recounted how music drew him into the mystery of the divine: "When the first notes of Mozart's Coronation Mass sounded, Heaven virtually opened and the presence of the Lord was experienced very profoundly."[61] Earlier, in his article "Wounded by the Arrow of Beauty," Cardinal Ratzinger describes attending a concert conducted by celebrated American composer Leonard Bernstein:

> I was sitting next to the Lutheran Bishop Hanselmann. After the last note of one of the great Thomas Kantor cantatas triumphantly faded away, we looked at each other spontaneously and just as spontaneously said: "Anyone who has heard this knows that the faith is true."[62]

Beauty and its artistic expression was not something trivial for Benedict XVI. He reminded the artists of their responsibility as "custodians of beauty." Expressing the true, the good, and the beautiful in their work elevates the culture around them and acknowledges that art efficaciously evokes the divine, "whose beauty comes in truth itself."

Benedict's efforts to bridge the human and the divine looked to the artistic realm as a vital arena for possibilities of metanoia. "The only really effective apologia for Christianity comes down to two arguments, namely, the *saints* the Church has produced and the *art* which has grown in her womb."[63] But what culture produced in the decades after the Second Vatican Council showed an explosive, perhaps deliberate, turn from the sacred to the profane. As explicitness prevailed, mystery vanished. This left little room for new Michelangelos or Dantes.

---

[61] "Pope Benedict's Words After Receiving Honorary Doctorate in Castel Gandolfo," *Zenit*, July 6, 2015, accessed November 3, 2015, http://www.zenit.org/.

[62] Joseph Ratzinger, "Wounded by the Arrow of Beauty" in *On the Way to Jesus Christ* (San Francisco: Ignatius Press, 2005), 37.

[63] Ratzinger with Messori, *Ratzinger Report*, 129.

Although there was no lack of distinctly Christian fare on the artistic landscape, works created by the likes of Bernini, Bach, or Flannery O'Connor were replaced with saccharine low-budget Christian movies and self-help books offering "prosperity theology." Reversing this was the impetus behind the Pontiff's meeting with artists. "The world in which we live runs the risk of being altered beyond recognition because of unwise human actions which, instead of beauty, unscrupulously exploit its resources for the advantage of a few and not infrequently disfigure the marvels of nature," he observed.[64] Art can alter cultural aesthetics, he believed. In evoking beauty, art inevitably evokes God. Here the Pope cited Simone Weil: "Beauty is the experimental proof that incarnation is possible."

During the meeting, Benedict could not help drawing attention to the wonders of Michelangelo encompassing them, particularly the fresco of the Last Judgment. "The fresco issues a strong prophetic cry against evil, against every form of injustice." And speaking of Michelangelo's artistic style, he continues, "The dramatic beauty of Michelangelo's painting, its colors and forms, becomes a proclamation of hope, an invitation to raise our gaze to the ultimate horizon."

Ignoring the ultimate horizon is the difference between the art of today and that of Michelangelo. Recapturing beauty has proven to be a quixotic undertaking in the age of relativism. Unlike the adventures of Lewis and Tolkien, or the beauty of Gregorian chant and Gothic architecture, very little today succeeds in drawing audiences out of their routines and into the transcendent—both in art and in religious ritual. All must be easily digested, predictable, and affordable. This leaves no room

---

[64] Benedict XVI, meeting with artists, November 21, 2009.

for the demands of the ultimate horizon. For Benedict, Michelangelo's achievements epitomized the search for the ultimate horizon, which sacred art should strive to convey: "Michelangelo presents to our gaze the Alpha and the Omega, the Beginning and the End of history, and he invites us to walk the path of life with joy, courage and hope."

The ultimate horizon is the encounter with the divine. "For believers, the Risen Christ is the Way, the Truth and the Life. For his faithful followers, he is the Door through which we are brought to that 'face-to-face' vision of God from which limitless, full and definitive happiness flows," Benedict said to the artists. Art's function in contemporary culture focuses on mankind's own achievement and accomplishment, or its weakness and bleakness. Its tales of anti-heroes who are nominally faithless or apathetic are wrapped in themes (sin, guilt, human failings) that owe just as much to Christianity as to the human person they explore. "The Church needs art," John Paul II voiced. "Does art need the Church?"[65]

In this meeting with artists, Benedict reaffirmed the artistic vocation of a "*via pulchritudinis*, a path of beauty which is at the same time an artistic and aesthetic journey, a journey of faith, of theological enquiry." Benedict implied that all the faithful, regardless of their vocation, are on the same path of beauty. The artists are the ones gifted with the task of journeying into areas where the theologian cannot. Yet even Benedict can be seen as a visionary seeking truth. We can only speculate as to what kind of artist Joseph Ratzinger might have become. A writer, like Leon Bloy, Georges Bernanos, or Fyodor Dostoevsky? A musician, making sense of God's placement in the modern world

---

[65] John Paul II, "Letter to Artists," April 4, 1999.

by German musical intonations? Or a man of letters, like Blaise
Pascal, Hilaire Belloc, or Josef Pieper? Certainly, not to comment on the world he saw around him would be unthinkable for
whatever profession Ratzinger might have chosen.

And yet it is impossible to separate Joseph Ratzinger from
the priest he became. No other vocational scenario fits. And it
was enough to concern himself with the beauty of the story of
the God-man. The ancient myths intuited Him in their imagi-
native ways, but without the poignancy and humbleness of His
impoverished beginnings or the humility that permeated His
life and the ongoing devotion it spawned. Ratzinger chose to
immerse himself in the story of Christ and His universal mission
rather than dedicate his life to his own artistic creations. And in
his vocation, that beauty influenced his thoughts, writings, and
words. To read Father Joseph Ratzinger is to see the unceasing
grace of the Holy Spirit's artistry.

It has become something of a tradition to conclude a major
papal document with a Marian prayer of intercession. In his
landmark treatise on modernism, *Pascendi Dominici Gregis*, Pope
Saint Pius X invoked the protection of "the Immaculate Virgin,
the destroyer of all heresies." In the Second Vatican Council's
Dogmatic Constitution on the Church, *Lumen Gentium*, the
Council Fathers implore Mary's powerful intervention before
her Son "until all families of people, whether they are honored
with the title of Christian or whether they still do not know
the Saviour, may be happily gathered together in peace and
harmony into one people of God." But it was John Paul II who
routinely invoked Mary, the Mother of God, as the ultimate
channel of prayer, from his first encyclical in 1979, *Redemptor*

Hominis, through his last completed writing as pontiff, *Ecclesia de Eucharistia*, in 2003.

Mary's influence on the life of faith of the universal Church is also prevalent in the path Joseph Ratzinger set out for himself and others over decades. Benedict XVI honed in on a Marian-themed pontificate precisely because he saw her vital role in salvation history as the human instrument that made possible the Incarnation. Ratzinger infused his meditations with a Marian shade, always invoking her prayers, always mindful of her as a model.

> Mary does not stop at a first superficial understanding of what is happening in her life, but can look in depth, she lets herself be called into question by events, digests them, discerns them, and attains the understanding that only faith can provide. It is the profound humility of the obedient faith of Mary, who welcomes within her even what she does not understand in God's action, leaving it to God to open her mind and heart.[66]

Mary also embodied the harmony of freedom and obedience, a central Ratzingerian theme. Her *fiat*—"let it be done to me"—is the prime example of the human person's free will oriented to the greater good. Her joy in being "full of grace" inspires us to turn away from sin and live in greater purity of heart.

Saint Luke's depiction of Mary in his Gospel has inspired reflections of beauty in art and writing throughout the ages. Her canticle is an image of her own joy: "My soul magnifies the Lord" (Luke 1:46). "To magnify the Lord means, not to want to magnify ourselves, our own name, our own ego; not to spread ourselves

---

[66] Benedict XVI, General Audience, December 19, 2012.

and take up more space, but to give him room so that he may be more present in the world," Cardinal Ratzinger writes.[67]

In the conclusion of his first encyclical, *Deus Caritas Est*, Benedict XVI continues John Paul II's tradition of a final petition to the Blessed Mother. Here, Benedict goes further. First, he draws on his earlier belief that the Church's great witness is in her saints. He reiterates Mary's supreme status among all the saints and confirms her own prophecy that "all generations will call me blessed" (Luke 1:48) as well as Jesus' words from the Cross, "Behold, your mother!" (John 19:27). Every succeeding generation has found in Mary unfailing matronly protection. "The testimonials of gratitude, offered to her from every continent and culture, are a recognition of that pure love which is not self-seeking but simply benevolent," Benedict writes, referencing the vibrant Marian devotions that have shaped the cultures of large parts of the world.[68]

And in poetic strokes Benedict offers a prayer to Mary that encompasses his particular vision for the faithful and the world at such a time, yearning for the motherly love that only Mary can provide. It also indicates Joseph Ratzinger's own artistic talent, directed always toward the greater picture—God. Just like Mary:

> Holy Mary, Mother of God,
> you have given the world its true light,
> Jesus, your Son—the Son of God.
> You abandoned yourself completely
> to God's call
> and thus became a wellspring

---

[67] Joseph Ratzinger, *Mary: Church at the Source* (San Francisco: Ignatius Press, 2005), 68.

[68] Benedict XVI, *Deus Caritas Est*, December 25, 2005, no. 42.

of the goodness which flows forth from him.
Show us Jesus. Lead us to him.
Teach us to know and love him,
so that we too can become
capable of true love
and be fountains of living water
in the midst of a thirsting world.[69]

Benedict largely impacted the Catholic intellectual tradition with his lifetime witness to the fruits of the Church, but his wisdom emerged as its own art form. It is a kind of poetry, as evident in his testament to the beauty of the unconditional love of the Creator and the human vessels chosen to introduce Him to others. A Ratzinger way of beauty, a *via pulchritudinis*, became clear, and the Face of which the prophets sang awaited its travelers.

It is the quest for this Face to which we now turn.

---

[69] Ibid.

CHAPTER FIVE

SEEKING THE HOLY FACE

*What did Jesus actually bring, if not world peace, universal
prosperity, and a better world? What has he brought?*

—Benedict XVI, *Jesus of Nazareth: From the Baptism
in the Jordan to the Transfiguration*

In his miniseries *Jesus of Nazareth*, director Franco Zeffirelli portrays Jesus asking His apostles, "Who do you say that I am?" (cf. Matt. 16:15). The camera pans from one silent apostle to another and ends on Simon Bar-Jonah (James Farentino), who finds himself answering, "You are the Messiah" (cf. Matt. 16:16).

In spite of Peter's confession, Christ's question continues to befuddle people. "But who do *you* say that I am?" And in the range of competing answers given, one definitive agreement emerges: Jesus of Nazareth continues to fascinate. As one author suggests, however, the variations that have emerged in the pursuit of the "historical Jesus" reflect the individual and the agenda formulating them.

Joseph Ratzinger was so concerned with this that he saw it as his final literary mission to present to the public a comprehensive study of Jesus that is intellectually rigorous and does not talk down to its audience. His final theological treatise, the *Jesus of Nazareth* trilogy, is Benedict's contribution to reintroducing the world to the Holy Face. Undertaken less as a personal achievement and more as a matter of duty, *Jesus of Nazareth* is the attempt from a theologian-bishop to counter the cultural hijacking of the figure of Jesus he saw unfolding around him. "Intimate friendship with Jesus," he wrote in the first volume's foreword, "on which everything depends, is in danger of clutching at thin air."[70]

Marked with the sign of faith, Joseph Ratzinger set out on the journey to reintroduce the world to the real Jesus. The Letter to the Colossians says of Christ: "He is the image of the invisible God, the firstborn of all creation" (1:15), but the familiarity to the modern ear of this Pauline language and tone flattens both the audacity and magnitude of such poetry. How to reclaim that wonder and awe? In this one line from Colossians, the Incarnation becomes less a matter of doctrine than a point of origin. In the birth of Jesus of Nazareth, the human face of God was finally unveiled. This reality breathed life into Joseph Ratzinger, who saw the grace given him as a calling to share it with others.

For years, the future pope pondered: How can Jesus speak to people today?

"If we had to choose today, would Jesus of Nazareth, the Son of Mary, the Son of the Father, have a chance? Do we really know Jesus at all? Do we understand him? Do we not perhaps have to make an effort to get to know him all over again?"[71]

---

[70] Benedict XVI, *Jesus of Nazareth: From the Baptism in the Jordan to the Transfiguration* (San Francisco: Ignatius Press, 2007), xii.

[71] Ibid., 41.

Although many invoke the name of Jesus, they fail to make a spiritual connection with Him. In our time, "[Jesus] is transformed from the 'Lord' (a word that is avoided) into a man who is nothing more than the advocate of all men."[72] Indeed, even for the faithful Christian, the mention of Jesus can become a cliché, such as on billboards urging travelers to repent in His name. In today's feel-good Christianity, the only basis for conscience is to ask what Jesus would do.

In our culture today, there is a spiritual aching and a longing for authenticity to shatter pervading cynicism. This longing cannot be satisfied by the many institutions or relationships that have failed to meet our spiritual needs. During his life and especially during his papacy, Benedict was intent on leading people to the real Jesus. The One he met was someone very different from the one championed by the pervading winds of that day.

Benedict reminded us that when "the Creator of heaven and earth" took on human form, He emerged not as a thundering conqueror, as the zealots would have hoped. He emerged as the personification of perfect love and truth in the completely original person of Jesus. "For the Son of man also came not to be served but to serve, and to give his life as a ransom for many" (Mark 10:45).

During his weekly series in 2006, Pope Benedict devoted an audience to each one of the apostles. Three incidents that Benedict expounds on involving Philip and Jesus' identity speak to us today in our search.

First, after accepting Jesus' call to follow Him, Philip encounters his dubious friend Nathanael. To Philip's glowing account of meeting Jesus, Nathanael retorts, "Can anything good come

---

[72] Ratzinger, *On the Way*, 8.

from Nazareth?" Philip's response is an invitation that beckons us as much as it did Nathanael: "Come and see" (John 1:46). Here, Benedict points out that these two verbs "imply personal involvement. The Apostle [Philip] engages us to become closely acquainted with Jesus."[73] Just as with any relationship, nurturing intimacy is required for such personal involvement.

Later, Philip serves as the conduit for "some Greeks" who wished to see Jesus (John 12:20–21). This encounter took on a legendary status in the early Church, specifically involving the Holy Face of Christ, a phenomenon we will explore shortly.[74] For now, however, the incident is an example of both evangelization and witness: "Each one of us must be an open road toward him!"[75] Benedict writes that in this seemingly innocuous request from Greek pilgrims to see Jesus, their desire is soon to be answered in more ways than they imagined: "In the crucified Jesus they will find the true God, the one they were seeking in their myths and their philosophy."[76]

Finally, during the Last Supper, Philip, probably with nothing but the best intention in mind, pleads, "Lord, show us the Father, and we shall be satisfied" (John 14:8). The disappointed reply reveals how obstinate the apostles' understanding must have been. "Have I been with you so long, and yet you do not know me, Philip? He who has seen me has seen the Father; how can you say, 'Show us the Father'? Do you not believe that I am in the Father and the Father in me? The words that I say to you

---

[73] Benedict XVI, General Audience, September 6, 2006.

[74] For a detailed study on this passage concerning the Greeks and the Face of Jesus, see Joseph Ratzinger, *The Spirit of the Liturgy* (San Francisco: Ignatius Press, 2000), 119.

[75] Benedict XVI, General Audience, September 6, 2006.

[76] Benedict XVI, *Jesus of Nazareth: Holy Week*, 18.

I do not speak on my own authority; but the Father who dwells in me does his works. Believe me that I am in the Father and the Father in me; or else believe me for the sake of the works themselves" (John 14:9–11).

Here we recall the words from Father Ratzinger's 1973 sermon quoted earlier: "He is a Person, and he seeks the person. He has a face, and he seeks our face."[77] Jesus' impassioned reply to Philip—"He who has seen me has seen the Father"—quite clearly indicates that there is no more denying who Jesus is, for the apostles or for us. "If we truly want to know the Face of God," Benedict said, "all we have to do is to contemplate the Face of Jesus! In his Face we truly see who God is and what he looks like!"[78]

In the opening of the Pope's first encyclical, which will be examined in the next chapter, Benedict succinctly details what it means to live an authentic life in faith:

> Being Christian is not the result of an ethical choice or a lofty idea, but the encounter with an event, a person, which gives life a new horizon and a decisive direction.[79]

A Transfigured Face

"He is the image of the invisible God" (Col. 1:15). The mystery of God in the form of man as Jesus of Nazareth is an awesome notion to contemplate. It is almost too mind-boggling, too far-fetched to grasp, and too big for an intimate friendship. And yet we are called to contemplate that mystery in prayer. We can do this through our imagination. We can picture ourselves as a character in a Gospel scene—perhaps a witness to Philip's invitation,

[77] Ratzinger, *God of Jesus Christ*, 24.
[78] Benedict XVI, General Audience, September 6, 2006.
[79] Benedict XVI, *Deus caritas est*, no. 1.

"Come and see," or a recipient of Paul's compelling letters. We might imagine joining Peter, James, and John on Mount Tabor to see Jesus transfigured (Matt. 17:2). Such use of the imagination in reading Scripture is part of *lectio divina* (holy reading), a method that Pope Benedict was convinced could usher in "a new spiritual springtime."[80]

What did the face of Jesus look like? What is the face of God to us today? The words of Benedict XVI and of his predecessor and his successor contain a startling number of references to "the face of God" and the exhortation to rediscover it anew in our time.

On one hand, the modern allusions to seeking out "the face of God" echo the longing of the psalmist, whose desire to gaze upon God's face spans the book of Psalms. That longing dominates the Old Testament.

John Paul II mentioned this Holy Face throughout his nearly twenty-seven-year pontificate.[81] In his penultimate trip out of Italy, to Bern, Switzerland in 2004, he said to the young Swiss Catholics:

> Christianity is not just a book of culture or an ideology, nor is it merely a system of values or principles, however lofty they may be. *Christianity is a person*, a presence, a face: Jesus, who gives meaning and fullness to human life.[82]

---

[80] Benedict XVI, "To the Participants in the International Congress Organized to Commemorate the 40th Anniversary of the Dogmatic Constitution on Divine Revelation, *Dei Verbum*," September 16, 2005.

[81] For example, Rino Fischella, "The Face of Christ," June 9, 2001, https://www.ewtn.com/library/Theology/FACECHRI.HTM.

[82] John Paul II, On the occasion of the national meeting of the young Catholics of Switzerland," June 5, 2004. Also, "Pope

In one of his final general audiences wherein he used the word "face" more than thirty times, Pope Benedict said, "Jesus does not tell us something about God, he does not merely speak of the Father but is the Revelation of God, because he is God and thus reveals the face of God."[83]

A few years later, Pope Francis would proclaim the Extraordinary Jubilee of Mercy for 2015–2016 with the papal bull entitled, *Misericordiae Vultus*, "The Face of Mercy." In the testament's opening line he wrote, "Jesus Christ is the face of the Father's mercy."

> The Church feels the urgent need to proclaim God's mercy. She knows that her primary task, especially at a moment full of great hopes and signs of contradiction, is to introduce everyone to the great mystery of God's mercy by contemplating the face of Christ.[84]

On the other hand, this same urgency compelled Joseph Ratzinger to write *Jesus of Nazareth* when he did: "It struck me as the most urgent priority to present the figure and message of Jesus in his public ministry."[85]

Is it more than a coincidence that this urgency comes in today's addicted age of multimedia, where one's virtual existence is in faces, pictures, the emphasis on the *ego* ("I") in the age of *video* ("to see")? Yet such a mania was predated by the joyous depiction of the God who became man, through countless artistic renderings of the face of Christ. Does not the age of the profile

---

Meets Youth Catholics of Switzerland," YouTube video, 1:08, posted by "AP Archive," July 21, 2015, https://www.youtube.com/watch?v=HWuVDBOHq3g.

[83] Benedict XVI, General Audience, January 16, 2013.

[84] Francis, *Misericordiae Vultus*, April 11, 2015, no. 25.

[85] Benedict XVI, *Jesus of Nazareth*, xxiv.

picture find its ancestor in the image of Christ's face on the veil of Veronica (*vera ikon*, "true image")?

The spread of Christianity truly marked a revolution. This was made evident in the plethora of depictions of the face of Christ in frescoes and mosaics—the rise of the icon. The effect of these images was explosive, bursting open the old Jewish prohibition against images. Iconoclast controversies ensued, and emperors and prelates rose and fell because of it.[86] The icon's stature—or rather the endurance of the face the icon depicts—remains with us, from the face of Jesus in the Hagia Sophia to the captivating legacy of the Shroud of Turin.

The Crossroads of Human Existence

Jesus of Nazareth: From the Baptism in the Jordan to the Transfiguration (2007) concerns itself with the public ministry of Jesus. The second volume, *Holy Week: From the Entrance into Jerusalem to the Resurrection* (2011), is a self-contained meditation on the final accounts of Jesus in the Gospels. Both speak to readers with the insights of a master theologian and the directness of a good pastor. With the final installment, *The Infancy Narratives* (2012), the trilogy—and, according to Archbishop Georg Gänswein—the theological output of Joseph Ratzinger and Benedict XVI finally concludes.[87]

Throughout the three works, Benedict brings the world of the Gospel directly into our world so that we can no longer cordon off Jesus in the past or in a theological vacuum. For instance, in

---

[86] See Christoph Schönborn, *God's Human Face* (San Francisco: Ignatius Press, 1994).

[87] Edward Pentin, "Jesus of Nazareth Concluded Benedict XVI's Theological Work, Secretary Says," *National Catholic Register*, March 23, 2015.

his explication of Jesus' temptations in the desert, Benedict brings to the forefront the source of miracles and the ultimate challenge to the powerful. In the devil's urging Jesus to throw Himself off the Temple to gain worldly splendor, Benedict sees the root of the pervading mentality that biblical interpretation is relative.[88]

"Christ did not cast himself down from the pinnacle. He did not tempt God. But he did descend into the abyss of death, into the night of abandonment, and into the desolation of the defenseless."[89] The desire to give in and be rescued by angels returned at Christ's darkest hour in the Garden of Gethsemane. "Abba, Father ... remove this cup from me" (Mark 14:36). In the second volume of *Jesus of Nazareth*, Pope Benedict offers a stark picture of what Jesus endured in that hour:

> Because he is the Son, he sees with total clarity the whole foul flood of evil, all the power of lies and pride, all the wiles and cruelty of the evil that makes itself as life yet constantly serves to destroy, debase, and crush life. Because he is the Son, he experiences all the horror, filth, and baseness that he must drink from the "chalice" prepared for him: the vast power of sin and death.[90]

Quoting from Blaise Pascal's *Pensées*, Benedict again places us within the Gospel: "We may see ourselves drawn quite personally: my own sin was present in that terrifying chalice. 'Those drops of blood I shed for you', Pascal hears the Lord say to him during the agony on the Mount of Olives."[91]

---

[88] Benedict XVI, *Jesus of Nazareth*, 37.
[89] Ibid., 38.
[90] Benedict XVI, *Jesus of Nazareth: Holy Week*, 155.
[91] Ibid., 156. Joseph Ratzinger often quoted Blaise Pascal (1623–1662). After a profound religious experience at age thirty-one,

Again and again, God's cause seems to be in its death throes. Yet over and over again it proves to be the thing that truly endures and saves. The earthly kingdoms that Satan was able to put before the Lord at that time have all passed away. Their glory, their *doxa*, has proven to be a mere semblance. But the glory of Christ, the humble, self-sacrificing glory of his love, has not passed away, nor will it ever do so.[92]

Despite all the evil around us, Jesus Christ — Love in the flesh — brought God, who is Light from Light, into the world. Despite our own sins that led to the death of Christ, His resurrection gives us hope:

With the resurrection of Jesus, light itself is created anew. He draws all of us after him into the new light of the resurrection and he conquers all darkness.... But how is this to come about? How does all this affect us so that instead of remaining word it becomes a reality that draws us in? Through the sacrament of baptism and the profession of faith, the Lord has built a bridge across to us, through which the new day reaches us. The Lord says to the newly-baptized: *Fiat lux* — let there be light. God's new day — the day of indestructible life, comes also to us. Christ takes you by the hand. From now on

Pascal wrote the fragmented apologetic work *Pensées*, out of which appeared the segment now known as Pascal's Wager. See Peter Kreeft, *Christianity for Modern Pagans: Pascal's Pensées* (San Francisco: Ignatius Press, 1993).

[92] Benedict XVI, *Jesus of Nazareth*, 44.

you are held by him and walk with him into the light, into real life.

It was for this reason that the early Church called baptism *photismos—illumination*.[93] It is the beginning of our life in Christ.

[93] Ibid.

CHAPTER 6

BENEDICT'S ENCYCLICALS PREACH FAITH, HOPE, AND LOVE

In meeting with United States bishops during his voyage to America in April 2008, Pope Benedict was asked to reflect on "a certain quiet attrition" that is seeing a pervading loss of faith sweeping the globe and various definitions of what "being Catholic" means today. Churches are closing, vocations fading, religious orders vanishing, and, to many, quaint Catholic customs and teachings struggling against the authorities of science, reason, and personal autonomy. In terms of sheer numbers the New Evangelization seems destined not to have the effect Benedict had hoped.

Such a situation was envisioned as early as 1970 by Joseph Ratzinger: "The reduction in the number of faithful will lead to [the Church] losing an important part of its social privileges. It will become small and will have to start pretty much all over again."[94] Joseph Ratzinger saw the crisis coming, and as Pope

---

[94] *Faith and the Future*, 116.

Benedict he had a thorough grasp of what is leading to the abandonment of our Catholic Faith.

But he would not abandon the people entrusted to his care. When he set out to write his encyclicals, Benedict saw a world yearning for authentic freedom, justice, and happiness, but it was failing to achieve these things by human hands alone. With his two completed letters on the theological virtues, *Deus Caritas Est*, on love, and *Spe Salvi*, on hope, the Pope gives us a vision of a more authentic world and presents signposts of truth that have the capacity to reshape mankind's trajectory in this very day and time.

"I wish in my first encyclical to speak of the love which God lavishes upon us," Benedict XVI stated in the introduction to *Deus Caritas Est* (*God Is Love*), "and which we in turn must share with others." It was not the type of inaugural encyclical that was expected from the newly elected pope who just spent nearly a quarter of a century as the cardinal prefect for the Congregation of the Doctrine of the Faith. Pope Benedict's decision to release *Deus Caritas Est* indicated a sublime message: this will not be a sweeping papacy of ambitious theological pursuits geared to showcase Joseph Ratzinger's intellectual command, but rather a return to the basics, to rebuild the fundamentals so that the Christian culture may be renewed and healed in its vocation to love and able to become again a beacon of hope in a world of darkness.

Deus Caritas Est addressed how love is perceived today, seeking to restore the timelessness and boundless understanding of love—the love of God, of Jesus Christ, and His Church. As the world struggles with the pain of divorce, chooses adolescence in lieu of adulthood, and believes the lies propagated by the hookup culture and pornography, Benedict shows us that the alternative—Christianity—has been neither properly communicated nor properly understood: "Doesn't the Church, with all her commandments and prohibitions, turn to bitterness the most precious thing in life? Doesn't she blow the whistle just when the joy which is the Creator's gift offers us a happiness which is itself a certain foretaste of the Divine?"[95] At the same time, Benedict is no less honest about the relativism that prevents an understanding of love: "For having reduced *eros* to pure 'sex,' it becomes a commodity, 'a thing' to be bought and sold, or rather, man himself becomes a commodity."[96]

Seeking inspiration to reintroduce love to a public growing ever more cynical, Pope Benedict looked to the height of Christian poetry—Dante Alighieri's *La Divina Comedia*. Recognizing that "today, the word 'love' is so spoiled, worn out and abused that one almost fears to pronounce it," the Pope "wanted to try to express for our time and our existence some of what Dante boldly summed up in his vision." In canto 33 of *Paradiso*, Dante describes the celestial light of a Trinitarian circle in which appeared "a human face—the face of Jesus Christ. God infinite light, has a human face and—we may add—a human heart."[97] Dante marvels in that canto, "Whoever sees that Light is soon made such that it would be impossible for him to set that Light aside for other sight; because the good, the object of the will, is fully gathered in that Light."[98] This is the "Light from Light," the

---

[95] Benedict XVI, *Deus Caritas Est*, no. 3.

[96] Ibid., no. 5.

[97] Benedict XVI, address to the participants at the meeting promoted by the Pontifical Council "Cor Unum," January 23, 2006. See also Paul Badde, *The Face of God*, 27–28.

[98] Dante Alighieri, *The Divine Comedy*, trans. Allen Mandelbaum (New York: Random House, 1995), 100–104.

incarnate Love "born of the Father before all ages," now entering our midst. "In this Encyclical, the themes 'God', 'Christ' and 'Love' are fused together as the central guide of Christian faith," Benedict describes.[99] The witness to the love of God as revealed in Christ lay at the heart of Benedict's intentions in *Deus Caritas Est*.

Benedict begins his encyclical by revealing that Saint John's statement of faith, "God is love" (1 John 4:8), not only was fulfilled in the person of Jesus Christ, but *is* Jesus Christ. In *Deus Caritas Est* and elsewhere in Ratzinger's canon, we glimpse the remarkable love story between God and man. It was out of unconditional love that God became fully human and lived among us. He had to show us how to love, even if it meant death. Indeed, it did mean death (cf. Gal. 4:4–5). Benedict explains that the Crucifixion was not just the matter in which He died; it was "love in its most radical form," unconditional love itself.[100]

For us, showing this same unconditional love to God and neighbor is possible because God made us: "Love is possible, and we are able to practice it because we are created in the image of God."[101]

In a passage in *Introduction to Christianity*, Professor Ratzinger shows how Jesus both actualizes unconditional love and is a model for manhood. Today, in a time of absent fathers, Ratzinger personalizes the Creedal axiom "and became man," explaining that man is meant to live for the other. Man is true man by sacrificing his desires for the well-being of those he loves. For the priest, it is a duty to the faithful entrusted to him; for those in marriage, a duty to wife and family; for the single and widowed,

---

[99] Benedict XVI, address at "Cor Unum" meeting.
[100] Benedict XVI, *Deus Caritas Est*, no. 12.
[101] Ibid., no. 39.

an openness to respond where one is needed. "Man is man by reaching out infinitely beyond himself, and he is consequently more of a man the less enclosed he is in himself, the less 'limited' he is."[102] The presence of Jesus in our midst blows open the enclosed, limited existence of choosing individualism over the other, selfishness over selflessness: "We have come to know and to believe in the love God has for us" (1 John 4:16).

The cult of individualism leaves in its wake not hope and joy, but sadness and cynicism. "In the end all that counts is one's own interest."[103] This is the legacy of Adam's desire to be like God (cf. Gen. 3:5). But Jesus is the new Adam. He is not meant to be a model beyond one's grasp, "an absolute exception, a curiosity, in which God demonstrates to us what sort of things are possible. His existence concerns all mankind."[104] Jesus shows us man's mission to live and love. His obedience to God's will—"not my will, but yours be done" (Luke 22:42)—becomes the will of God; the two are not opposed but linked. Jesus demonstrates that the role of man is not omnipotence but sonship; it is obedience to the needs of others. As adopted sons and daughters of God, we become the Body of Christ. This is what Benedict means when he tells us that faith is not solely a private experience, but demands interrelationships. It also illustrates the essence of *eros, philia,* and *agape*: union with the other. "We become 'one body', completely joined in a single existence. Love of God and love of neighbor are now truly united: God incarnate draws us all to himself."[105] Just as we yearn to share joyful moments and

---

[102] Ratzinger, *Introduction to Christianity*, 235.
[103] Benedict XVI, General Audience, December 3, 2008.
[104] Ratzinger, *Introduction to Christianity*, 236.
[105] Benedict, XVI, *Deus Caritas Est*, no. 14.

occurrences with another, so too is the intention of the ultimate fulfillment of the Kingdom of God: everlasting union in the light of love that Dante described and that Benedict seeks to reintroduce to us. He dares us to raise our eyes from the ground to the heights of eternal possibility.

But it does not come without a price. While on the Cross, Christ reached down into the depths of human existence so as to lift it up. This "descent into hell" leads us to ponder Benedict's next encyclical, *Spe Salvi*, "in hope we were saved" (Rom. 8:24).

In *Spe Salvi*, Benedict chose not to lament the passing of the old way of "ghettoized Catholicism" or to cower from secularism's agendas as mere signs of the times, or to dream of a utopian future apart from worldly problems. "Christian faith is not just a look back at what has happened in the past, an anchorage in an origin that lies behind us in time; nor is it just an outlook on the eternal; it is above all things a looking forward, a reaching-out of hope."[106]

Benedict points out that the concept of hope is not lacking in our time but is misplaced. The result is like Babel, where sin is not overcome but festers and each individual vies for his own idea of hope and his own desires.

Hope cannot be properly contemplated without returning to the Cross. To defy death, God in the person of Jesus took on the whole of human suffering. To each person who finds himself alone, suffering, abandoned, desperate, or proud and presumptuous, Jesus says: I am with you, and will raise you up.[107] Typically, Christ's descent into hell is viewed, if at all, as a remotely cosmological and theological phrase with little real meaning, when in

---

[106] Ratzinger, *Introduction to Christianity*, 242.

[107] See Josef Pieper, *Faith, Hope, Love*, (San Francisco: Ignatius Press, 1997), 113.

fact it is an assurance of solidarity, for all the living past, present, and future: even God descended into the depths, and now even those depths are bathed in His light.[108] The hell of the agony in the garden on Holy Thursday and of Good Friday and the silence of Holy Saturday all encompass this descent. "Christ descended into 'Hell' and is therefore close to those cast into it, transforming their darkness into light."[109] If the downtrodden do not have hope, what is hope other than selfish pursuit?

One of Joseph Ratzinger's favorite themes, "com-passion," which means "to suffer with," is applied here. Citing Saint Bernard of Clairvaux and reflecting on the Passion of Christ, Pope Benedict said: "God is love, and the deeper one's union with God, the more full one is of love. And though God cannot endure pain, he is not without compassion for those who do."[110]

Benedict then leaps beyond the theological into our everyday realities: "The true measure of humanity is essentially determined in relationship to suffering and to the sufferer." The reality and lasting significance of faith, hope, and love are meaningful only if they are lived. This message inevitably clashes with the temptation today to dispose of any person across life's spectrum considered unable to contribute to society, irrespective of how such contribution is defined or who defines it—relativism at its finest. "A society unable to accept its suffering members and incapable of helping to share their suffering and to bear it inwardly

---

[108] See de Lubac, *Catholicism*, 38, n. 13, quoting the ancient Syriac liturgy: "He visited Adam in Sheol—and brought him astonishing news—He promised him life—and the resurrection that would completely renew him."

[109] Benedict XVI, *Spe Salvi*, no. 41.

[110] Saint Bernard of Clairvaux, "Commentary on the Song of Songs," 26, 5; see also *Jesus of Nazareth*, 87 and *Spe Salvi*, no. 42.

through 'com-passion' is a cruel and inhuman society."[111] Here in *Spe Salvi*, Benedict makes it clear that our hope must not be individualistic. Rather, our priority must be the dignity and care for the body and soul of each individual. "A world which has to create its own justice is a world without hope."[112]

> The capacity to accept suffering for the sake of goodness, truth and justice is an essential criterion of humanity, because if my own well-being and safety are ultimately more important than truth and justice, then the power of the stronger prevails, then violence and untruth reign supreme.[113]

Benedict introduces the meaning of *con-solatio* — consolation — as "being with" the other. *Con-solatio* and *com-passion* form our life's purpose, which is to renounce self-love in order to see the essence of others.

✂ ✂ ✂

Pope Benedict XVI also considers the Last Judgment as key to understanding Christian hope. While it is only right to receive a just account of one's life — the doctrine of particular judgment — hope in the unconditional love of God leads one to pray for both compassion and consolation when facing final judgment: God's "mercy endures forever" (cf. Ps. 136). However, "Christ's mercy is not a grace that comes cheap, nor does it imply the trivialization of evil."[114] Belief in the Last Judgment coincides

---

[111] Benedict XVI, *Spe Salvi*, no. 38.
[112] Ibid., no. 42.
[113] Ibid., no. 38.
[114] Benedict XVI, homily during Mass "Pro Eligendo Romano Pontifice," April 18, 2005.

with anticipating the Kingdom of God: it is not something to be feared, but is lived in hope because "in hope we were saved." We who have lived in justice and truth can expect to be met with that same justice and truth in death.

Still, Benedict acknowledges the difficulty the majority of people face in forging an authentic life: "Much filth covers purity, but the thirst for purity remains and it still constantly re-emerges from all that is base and remains present in the soul. What happens to such individuals when they appear before the Judge?"[115] The Pope does not shy away from the image of passing through fire, quoting a startling passage from Paul: "Now if any one builds on the foundation with gold, silver, precious stones, wood, hay, stubble — each man's work will become manifest; for the Day will disclose it, because it will be revealed with fire" (1 Cor. 3:12–13). But then, as we have seen in this study on hope and love, although we may have to pass through the fire revealing the truth of our character, it can only be the fire of God we encounter, and thus the fire not of wrath but of mercy—the fire of love.

> This encounter with him, as it burns us, transforms and frees us, allowing us to become truly ourselves. All that we build during our lives can prove to be mere straw, pure bluster, and it collapses. Yet in the pain of this encounter, when the impurity and sickness of our lives become evident to us, there lies salvation. His gaze, the touch of his heart heals us through an undeniably painful transformation "as through fire". But it is a blessed pain, in which the holy power of his love sears through us like

[115] Benedict XVI, *Spe Salvi*, no. 46.

a flame, enabling us to become totally ourselves and thus totally of God.[116]

Such perspective is radical, even revolutionary.

At the World Meeting of Families in 2012, Pope Benedict recalled his childhood when prompted by a seven-year-old girl with her family from Vietnam. Even in the devastation wrought by the Nazi regime and in the aftereffects of the war, "the mutual love that we shared, our joy, even in simple things, was so strong that it enabled us to endure and overcome these things," Benedict recalled, linking simple and little things as an expression of warmheartedness. "And so we grew up convinced that it was good to be human, because we saw God's goodness reflected in our parents and our brothers and sisters."[117]

And given his future retirement and life of solitude that would follow his time as successor of Saint Peter, Pope Benedict disclosed to the gathered couples and families a personal, moving hope: "When I try to imagine what Heaven will be like, I think it must be like the time when I was a small boy. In this environment of trust, joy and love, we were happy, and I think that Heaven must be rather like those early years. So in a way, I am hoping to return 'home' when I leave 'for the other part of the world'."[118]

"May you see your Redeemer face-to-face," imparts the prayer for the dying. Benedict XVI shows us that although living out faith, hope, and love is not without its challenges, its reward is Someone who has been waiting for us all along. We are home.

[116] Benedict XVI, *Spe Salvi*, no. 47.
[117] Benedict XVI, address during Seventh World Meeting of Families, Bresso Park, June 2, 2012.
[118] Ibid.

CHAPTER SEVEN

A PERSONAL ENCOUNTER WITH THE DIVINE

Jerusalem

[Stephen] said, "Behold, I see the heavens opened, and
the Son of man standing at the right hand of God." But
they cried out with a loud voice and stopped their ears
and rushed together upon him. Then they cast him out
of the city and stoned him; and the witnesses laid down
their garments at the feet of a young man named Saul.
(Acts 7:55–58)

We are in the 30s of the first century, and the first martyr for
Christ, Stephen, has just been stoned as Saul of Tarsus stood by
and watched. Pope Benedict XVI teaches us that Saul, a Jew
who spoke Greek but was a Roman citizen, was about thirty at
the time. Saul studied under Rabbi Gamaliel of the Hillel school
and was a tentmaker by trade. This diverse life placed him "at the
intersection between three different cultures—Roman, Greek,

and Jewish"—and thus open "for a mediation between cultures, for true universality."[119]

But Saul of Tarsus felt no openness toward the burgeoning Christian movement dubbed "the Way," which worshipped the itinerant, crucified preacher Jesus of Nazareth. Saul "saw the new movement as a risk, a threat to the Jewish identity, to the true Orthodoxy of the fathers."[120] As the apostles of Jesus struggled to keep the message alive, "Saul was trying to destroy the church," arresting men and women and throwing them into prison (Acts 8:3). A violent force had overtaken him. Luke writes that Saul was "breathing threats and murder," a visceral image of rage and obsession (Acts 9:1). Saul was convinced that his zealotry was of and for God (Acts 22:3). But perhaps he could not shake an interior unease in the face of the calm testimonies of these followers of Jesus, of Stephen's willful abandonment to death, perhaps even the lingering face of this Jesus he had not even met.

"In raging fury against them, I persecuted them even to foreign cities," he himself later admits (Acts 26:11). This time, Saul set his eyes to the north, to Syria, where known associates of the Way established a community of believers (Acts 22:5). With the full commission and authority of the high priests to carry out his personal mission of purgation, Paul and some armed men set out for Damascus.

The Road to Damascus

What was Saul thinking during the long hours of his journey? Did he pray psalms, in accordance with his faith, the same hymns

---

[119] Benedict XVI, General Audience, August 27, 2008.
[120] Ibid.

sung by those he sought to persecute? Perhaps it was something more urgent: food, water, cleanliness. But comfort and Saul's own plan of life were about to end. The dusty, sunbaked road into Damascus gave way to the "well-tended green gardens lying all around the ancient city and the two rivers whose embrace made this plain a lovely place of rich harvest."[121]

He was so near to the city, he could see the outlines of the town. It was about noon (Acts 22:6ff.).

And then it happened.

✳ ✳✳ ✳

The conversion of Saul of Tarsus, who became Paul the Apostle, is not a moment unreachable for us. In fact, "Conversion was at the heart of the preaching of Jesus."[122] As it was with Paul, it is with all of us: conversion—from the Latin *convertere*, "to turn around"—is a conscious choice to change directions. It is the yes to God's invitation, even if at times, as in the case with Paul, that invitation felt like a blinding earthquake. All conversions are not as physically vivid as Paul's, but they are no less dramatic internally. And although Paul continued on to Damascus, he had been turned around profoundly. He could never go back in the same direction again. "I would to God that not only you but also all who hear me this day might become such as I am," Paul said before the court of King Agrippa in Caesarea, "except for these chains," (Acts 26:29). But Paul's real chains had long been broken, by the will of God—and by

[121] Fulton Oursler, "The Road to Damascus," in *A Treasury of Catholic Reading*, ed. John Chapin (New York: Farrar, Straus, and Cudahy, 1957).

[122] Weigel, *The End and the Beginning*, 511.

Paul's decision to accept it. "The courage to make the break gives you freedom," Joseph Ratzinger has said, "it alone gives freedom. This courage to make the break is called, in biblical language — *metanoia*."[123]

This intimate experience of metanoia is the pivotal, missing point in the loss of faith in modern times: the lack of desire for a personal encounter with the divine, for conversion itself, for Christ to be encountered. Faith will not grow where it is not nurtured. Even places of learning, so dear to Joseph Ratzinger, often seek to undermine rather than enhance the faith of believers, considering the faith relevant only as it pertains to classes in anthropology and the humanities. Benedict XVI emphasized this to his fellow bishops in Mexico: "Knowledge of the content of faith alone is never a substitute for the experience of a personal encounter with the Lord."[124]

Today, institutions, nations, and individuals are in need of conversion. Benedict XVI's mission has been to foster that conversion to set ablaze the globe with revolutions of faith.

Conversion is union with the will of God but requires a movement toward the ever-radiant light, something Paul forcefully discovered and spoke of time and again: "Examine yourselves, to see whether you are holding to your faith. Test yourselves. Do you not realize that Jesus Christ is in you?—unless indeed you fail to meet the test!" (2 Cor. 13:5).

Through Benedict's teaching, we see in Paul's conversion the radical nature of what conversion entails: Paul is thrown to the

---

[123] Joseph Ratzinger, "The Forgiveness of Sins: Metanoia as the Fundamental Datum of Christian Existence" in *Credo for Today* (San Francisco: Ignatius Press, 2009), 153.

[124] Benedict XVI, address to the bishops of Mexico on their *ad limina* visit, September 8, 2005.

ground, his plan is upended, he is blinded by light, and it is only later that the scales fall and his eyesight returns—but his perspective is anew. It is what is meant in the sacrament of Baptism: a conversion from an old life to a new one. "The dazzling radiance of the Risen Christ blinds him; thus what was his inner reality is also outwardly apparent, his blindness to the truth, to see the light that is Christ."[125] We also see again the original name for Baptism in the early Church, "'illumination,' because this Sacrament gives light; it truly makes one see."[126]

These lessons on Saint Paul encompass one of Pope Benedict's greatest triumphs—his weekly Wednesday general audiences. These audiences gave him the opportunity to delve into far-reaching matters of the Faith, to illustrate the still-present illumination of God in the world against pervading forces that seek to direct that light away from the truth to their own agendas. "When people are seized by love, a new dimension of being opens in them, a new grandeur and breadth of reality, and it also drives one to express oneself in a new way."[127]

Conversion, then, does not strip the converted of their freedom and force them into blind obedience. Instead, it leads to reconciliation and a dynamic relationship between Creator and being, opening the possibilities of one's life into exciting avenues. Benedict XVI was convinced that redemption never comes too late, and that only hardness of heart is an obstacle to the hope of "making the break."

---

[125] Benedict XVI, General Audience, September 3, 2008.
[126] Ibid.
[127] "Pope Benedict's Words After Receiving Honorary Doctorate in Castel Gandolfo," *Zenit*, July 6, 2015, https://zenit.org/.

To set right our relations with God

Is true conversion of heart a mystical moment relegated to the exceptional of history? So drastic have conversions been that names are changed, lives forever altered: Abram to Abraham, Simon to Peter, Saul to Paul, Edith Stein to Saint Teresa Benedicta of the Cross, Francesco Forgione to Saint Padre Pio, Anjezë Gonxhe Bojaxhiu to Saint Teresa of Calcutta. In his first audience after announcing his intention to retire, Benedict cited two quotations from Dorothy Day's autobiography that indicate her *metanoia* transformation: "I wanted to be with the protesters, go to jail, write, influence others and leave my dreams to the world," she writes. "How much ambition and how much searching for myself in all this!" While passionate for justice, she noticed her own ego was domineering everything. "But Grace acts nevertheless," Benedict comments, quoting her: "I felt the need to go to church more often, to kneel, to bow my head in prayer."[128] Referencing Revelation's "Behold, I stand at the door and knock" (Rev. 3:20), Benedict concludes his penultimate general audience by acknowledging the many conversions of those who were engulfed in a seemingly satisfied lifestyle and who unexpectedly—and often unwittingly—heard the knock. "Being converted means not shutting ourselves into the quest for our own success, our own prestige, our own status, but rather ensuring that every day, in the small things, truth, faith in God and love become the most important thing of all."[129]

Yet, the idea of conversion as conforming to doctrine persists. Hence the popular portrayal that the shrugging off of faith is the real path to enlightenment. This comes with the notion

---

[128] Benedict XVI, General Audience, February 13, 2016.
[129] Ibid.

that belief is a crutch, that science and reason alone are tools for discovery, and to many, that the blurring of morality is the absolute measure of life's experiences. But science can deal with only the known world, powerless in matters of the heart—or conversion. And the quest for pleasure and experience as the source of happiness hinges on fleeting moments rather than on genuine immersion with the other.

> Who is authentically growing as a man, who is advancing, going forward: the playboy who lurches from one fleeting encounter to the next and has no time at all to really encounter a "thou"? Or the man who carries through his Yes to another human being, goes forward with it, and in this Yes actually does not become rigid but rather learns slowly and ever more deeply therein to make himself available to the "thou" and thus actually to find freedom, truth, and love? Just to continue that Yes, once it is spoken, demands a constant willingness to change, one that makes a person mature.[130]

"In the two kinds of change that are contrasted here," Cardinal Ratzinger continues, "it seems to me that the authenticity of the Christian willingness to change is clearly evident over against the 'cult of movement'." He observes the politicization of what is meant by "change," that "change" and "progress" are the only means of salvation, and that as religious faith erodes, political faith escalates.

> Salvation comes only through change; calling somebody a conservative is the equivalent of an excommunication

---

[130] Joseph Ratzinger, "Forgiveness of Sins," 156.

from society, because in current parlance it is tantamount to saying that he is opposed to progress, closed off from the new, and thus a defender of what is old, obscure, and servile, and enemy of the salvation that is expected from change. Does metanoia point in the same direction?[131]

"In order to become a Christian," Joseph Ratzinger summarizes, "a human being must change, not merely in one place or another, but unconditionally, down to the very bottom of his being."[132] This change demands not blind subjugation to dogma but a living embodiment of a code of life, a distinct *Way*—the very way of Jesus Christ. Franco Zeffirelli, before embarking on bringing first-century Jerusalem to life in *Jesus of Nazareth*, was alerted what would befall him in the process. "A priest friend who is dear to me warned that when you begin to involve yourself in godly matters it is terribly difficult to return to mundane trivialities."[133]

Such testimonies and experiences of altered lives to a transfigured faith indicate not only the legitimacy of the Christian proposal, but also the responsibility one has to its claims and graces. This is no one-and-done-deal, but an ongoing commitment, something foreign to the playboy's routine lifestyle in Cardinal Ratzinger's scenario. Such commitment is indeed rare, especially when under assault by rootlessness that longs to make malleable that which cannot change, not because of rigidity but because of the absolutes it professes.

---

[131] Benedict XVI, "Change and Fidelity," in *Credo for Today: What Christians Believe* (San Francisco: Ignatius Press, 2009).

[132] Ibid.

[133] Franco Zeffirelli, *Jesus—A Spiritual Diary* (New York: Harper and Row, 1984), 1.

The attempt to give Christianity new publicity value by setting it without qualification in a positive relation to the world, indeed, by portraying it as conversion to the world, suits our feelings about life and hence is becoming increasingly widespread.

A Christianity that regards proving its piety in all respects according to the standards of the day as its only remaining task has nothing to say and no importance. It can just step aside.[134]

Rather than retreating into a cloistered community, those who are converted to Christ speak and act with humble joy, compassion, and charity. Benedict believed that, like the saints, this is the best way to reach others and to offer them a convincing alternative to our culture.

"When the world goes wrong, it proves rather that the Church is right"[135] said Benedict. Such is the responsibility of the converted. "The only thing that can help Christianity is the prophetic courage to bring its own voice decisively and unmistakably to bear on the present hour."

Those who live in today's world with their eyes open, who recognize its contradictions and its destructive tendencies—from the self-defeating consequences of technology in polluting the environment to the self-defeating behavior of society in its problems with race and class—do not expect a Christian affirmation but rather the prophetic salt that stings, burns, accuses, and transforms. With

---

[134] "The Forgiveness of Sins," 144–145.
[135] G. K. Chesterton, *The Everlasting Man* (San Francisco: Ignatius Press, 2008), 10.

that, nevertheless, a fundamental aspect of metanoia has moved into our field of vision—for it requires a change in man in order for salvation to come about.[136]

And the portal wherein an honest account is offered, leading to an illuminated path of real enlightenment and joyful living is the sacrament of Penance. During his pontificate, Pope Benedict attempted to bridge the trepidation typically associated with approaching the sacrament, likening it to drawing from "the inexhaustible fountain of divine love." He continues, "Only from this spiritual source is it possible to draw the indispensable interior energy to overcome the evil and sin in the ceaseless battle that marks our earthly pilgrimage toward the heavenly homeland."[137] This striking imagery of a "ceaseless battle" between goodness and sin demonstrates that even the soul and conscience need renewal. Still, many see Confession as remote and archaic and believe that they can renew their souls or their consciences with other, less rigid exercises—ones that do not include confessing to a priest.

We must admit that in our individualistic age it has become enormously difficult for people to cross the threshold of personal confession. But where the spirit of faith is leading us, then it can be learned anew. Above all because this is not an admission of guilt before men, but before God, and ends with the word of forgiveness.[138]

---

[136] "The Forgiveness of Sins," 145–146.

[137] Benedict XVI, address to the participants in a course on the Internal Forum organized by the Tribunal of the Apostolic Penitentiary, March 16, 2007.

[138] Ratzinger with Seewald, *God and the World*, 422.

Even if one yearns for true metanoia and renewal, the process is never complete, and the need for Confession returns again and again. But how does one effectively approach it?

Pope Benedict tells us that we must possess an awareness of sin and discern its gravity—no easy task in today's culture, which has lost the sense of sin. But the Pope assures us that reconciliation with God is the priority, His mercy foremost. "Confession is only necessary in the case of serious sin," he said, adding, "Only when you are in a state of 'mortal' sin, grave sin, is it necessary to go to confession before Communion."[139] In this directive, Benedict pacifies the scrupulous, who feel the need to confess out of compulsion, and he also indicates the holiness of the Eucharist and the proper state in which we must approach it.

Secondly, the Pope understands that the penitent often confesses the same sins:

> It is true: our sins are always the same, but we clean our homes, our rooms, at least once a week, even if the dirt is always the same; in order to live in cleanliness, in order to start again. Otherwise, the dirt might not be seen but it builds up. Something similar can be said about the soul, for me myself: if I never go to confession, my soul is neglected and in the end I am always pleased with myself and no longer understand that I must always work hard to improve, that I must make progress.[140]

[139] Benedict XVI, address at a catechetical meeting with children who had received First Communion during the year, October 15, 2005.

[140] Ibid.

The act of facing one's sins, asking forgiveness to God, and setting out anew is both a physical and spiritual act. Entering the confessional is taking responsibility for one's actions.

During a pastoral visit to the Rebibbia Prison outside Rome, the Pope was asked by an inmate about absolution being "delegated to priests." "If I asked for it on my knees alone in my room, turning to the Lord, would he absolve me?" Responding that forgiveness indeed comes when one with true love asks for it, he expands further:

> Hold on to two dimensions: the vertical one, with God, and the horizontal one, with the community of the Church and humanity. The absolution of the priest, sacramental absolution, is necessary to really absolve me of this link with evil and to fully reintegrate me into the will of God, into the vision of God, into his Church and to give me sacramental, almost bodily, certitude: God forgives me, he receives me into the community of his children. I think that we must learn how to understand the Sacrament of Penance in this sense: as a possibility of finding again, almost physically, the goodness of the Lord, the certainty of reconciliation.[141]

Benedict XVI, who has always believed we are better people than we allow ourselves to be, invites us to allow ourselves the incredible peace that flows from absolution, as we hear the words of absolution.

Saint Benedict, whose name Joseph Ratzinger chose for his pontifical name, speaks eloquently and humbly of the continual

---

[141] Benedict XVI, responses to the questions posed by inmates, December 18, 2011.

rising and falling that marks the path of metanoia, the path of hope, the path of forgiveness and peace: "Always we begin again." The parable of the prodigal son is also the story of the unconditional love of the father, whose love radiates through whatever we have done; yet, it is up to each of us to make the break. The world needs healing, but this can be done only when each individual is willing to forgive others and has the desire for conversion, asserting with humble determination, "I *must* begin again."[142]

Like Saint Paul, who rose from the Damascus road a new man following his encounter with the Lord of Light, Benedict XVI's foray into godly matters reveals the heights to which conversion can take those who are willing to go through the bowels of the underworld and into that "ceaseless battle" between good and evil wearing "the whole armor of God, that [they] may be able to withstand in the evil day, and having done all, to stand" (Eph. 6:13).

---

[142] Benedict XVI, homily during a visit to Rome's prison for minors, March 18, 2007; emphasis mine.

CHAPTER EIGHT

FAREWELL TO THE DEVIL

*Now war arose in heaven, Michael and his angels fighting
against the dragon; and the dragon and his angels fought,
but they were defeated and there was no longer any place for
them in heaven. And the great dragon was thrown down,
that ancient serpent, who is called the Devil and Satan,
the deceiver of the whole world—he was thrown down to
the earth, and his angels were thrown down with him.*

—Revelation 12:7–9

For most of the twentieth century, Leo XIII's prayer to Saint
Michael was recited at the end of every Mass:

> Saint Michael, the Archangel,
> Defend us in battle.
> Be our protection against the wickedness
>   and snares of the devil.
> May God rebuke him, we humbly pray,
> And do thou, O Prince of the Heavenly Hosts,
> By the power of God, thrust into Hell Satan

and all the evil spirits, who roam about the
world seeking the ruin of souls. Amen.

The prayer was written in 1886, yet the language evokes images from the Middle Ages. Many people today might wonder
whether it would be better to put to rest the strange, disturbing
verbiage about Satan, the Antichrist, and eternal damnation so
that the Church would appear more attractive and welcoming.
Yet somehow, "in an age in which Christianity is supposed to be
the faith of reason, many are still fascinated by the possibility
of miracles, apparitions, encounters with the devil, and other
signs of the supernatural," writes John Thavis in *The Vatican
Prophecies*.[143]

Pope Francis himself is a vocal proponent of the reality of the
supernatural realm and the intent of "the evil one." Because he
recognizes that the power of the evil one is active in the world,
he consecrated Vatican City to the protection of Saint Michael
the Archangel and Saint Joseph. Pope Emeritus Benedict XVI's
attendance at this consecration accentuated its spiritual importance. This is an age of unbridled spiritual warfare, characterized
here on earth as the ongoing struggle between the "city of the
flesh" and the "city of the spirit," and in the otherworld as a
desperate assault by the forces of darkness seeking to undo the
forces of good.

And in this struggle immortal souls are at stake.

Whereas Francis has received wide press regarding his frequent
expositions of the devil's wily ways, Benedict XVI is not usually

---

[143] John Thavis, *The Vatican Prophecies* (New York: Viking, 2015), 2.

associated with discourses on the cosmic realm. Yet he has not shied from expressing the reality of spiritual warfare, and he is acutely aware of modern man's tongue-in-cheek view of the supernatural, particularly toward manifestations of evil. This awareness can be seen in his ongoing observation of the increasing intolerance for Christianity and the failure to recognize it as the foundation of ethics, law, and morality in the public square. In some ways, refusal to believe in the devil is inseparably linked with the rise of the "tyranny of relativism" (as Francis dubbed Ratzinger's phrase).

In the mid-nineteenth century, Charles Baudelaire included in his work "The Generous Gambler" the now-famous adage (also popularized in the film *The Usual Suspects*): "One of the devil's best ruses is to persuade you that he does not exist!" Ratzinger echoes this idea in his discussion with Vittorio Messori: "We must not yield to the mentality of so many believers nowadays who think it is enough to act more or less like the majority and everything will automatically be right."[144] We will examine the majority-rule mentality in a later chapter.

Ratzinger links the work of Satan with "the last things": death, judgment, heaven, and hell. Failing to ponder the conclusion of one's earthly existence has lowered the gaze and the expectation of the Catholic worldview. "Since many Christians have lost their sense for the 'last things', death is surrounded by silence, fear or the attempt to trivialize it."[145] Excising the presence of the evil one and of death as expectation of the coming of

---

[144] Ratzinger with Messori, *Ratzinger Report*, 144. See chapter 10, "On Some 'Last Things'" for insights from both Ratzinger and Messori that remain timely for today as when the dialogue occurred (ca. 1985).

[145] Ibid., 145.

Christ has weakened people's understanding of other elements, such as the Eucharist and the celebrations of Advent, Christmas, and Easter as ways of proclaiming *"Marana tha!"* "Come, Lord Jesus!" "Can we pray, therefore, for the coming of Jesus? Can we sincerely say: '*Marana tha!* Come, Lord Jesus!'? Yes, we can. And not only that: we must!"[146]

And so, combating "the father of lies" (John 8:44) is an essential element of the Christian journey. We see this in Scripture, such as demonic presences in the Gospels, the temptations of Jesus in the desert, and "Satan entering into" Judas (John 13:27); and in the Spiritual Exercises of Saint Ignatius of Loyola,[147] the testimonies of saints such as Padre Pio,[148] and the work of exorcists. We also see it in the reception of the sacraments, beginning with the baptismal vow to reject Satan.[149] We must be warriors against wickedness, strengthened by the virtues of faith, hope, and love.

During Benedict's Holy Land pilgrimage in 2009, Ephesians was a selected reading:

> Finally, be strong in the Lord and in the strength of his might. Put on the whole armor of God, that you may be able to stand against the wiles of the devil. For we are not contending against flesh and blood, but against the principalities, against the powers, against the world rulers of this

[146] Benedict XVI, *Jesus of Nazareth: Holy Week*, 292.

[147] William Barry, "The Devil Comes Cloaked as an Angel of Light," in *An Ignatian Spirituality Reader*, edited by George Traub (Chicago: Loyola Press, 2008).

[148] Andrea Monda, "A Troublesome Saint," *Inside the Vatican*, April 1999.

[149] See Joseph Ratzinger, "Farewell to the Devil?" in *Dogma and Preaching: Applying Christian Doctrine to Daily Life* (San Francisco: Ignatius Press, 2011).

present darkness, against the spiritual hosts of wickedness in the heavenly places. Therefore take the whole armor of God, that you may be able to withstand in the evil day, and having done all, to stand. (Eph. 6:10–13)

In the Holy Mass we are clothed with this armor of God. The liturgy, with its prayers, readings, and celebration of the Eucharist, "is the summit toward which the activity of the Church is directed; at the same time it is the font from which all her power flows."[150]

In *The Spirit of the Liturgy*, Ratzinger references the relationship between the meaning of the liturgy and the evil one. For instance, the Sign of the Cross, "the most basic Christian gesture," indicates many things in the faithful's relationship to God: an evocation of the Crucifixion, a confession of faith in the triune God, a remembrance of Baptism, a sign of Christ's Passion and Resurrection. In the Sign of the Cross, "the whole essence of Christianity is summed up."[151] The Cross is also a sign against the advances of evil. "It is, so to speak, the saving staff that God holds out to us, the bridge by which we can pass over the abyss of death, and all the threats of the Evil One, and reach God."[152]

The act of kneeling is another seemingly simple element Ratzinger mentions in *The Spirit of the Liturgy*. Genuflecting and kneeling in the liturgy are signs of adoration, a "theology of kneeling" found in Philippians 2:6–11: "at the name of Jesus

---

[150] Paul VI, *Sacrosanctum Concilium* (Constitution on the Sacred Liturgy), December 4, 1963.

[151] Joseph Ratzinger, *The Spirit of the Liturgy* (San Francisco: Ignatius Press, 2000), 177–178.

[152] Ibid.

every knee should bow, in heaven and on earth and under the earth" (Phil. 2:10). Ratzinger writes, "The Christian liturgy is a cosmic liturgy precisely because it bends the knee before the crucified and exalted Lord. Here is the center of authentic culture — the culture of truth."[153] He then relates an anecdote from the Desert Fathers:

> The devil was compelled by God to show himself to a certain Abba Apollo. He looked black and ugly, with frighteningly thin limbs, but, most strikingly, *he had no knees*. The inability to kneel is seen as the very essence of the diabolical.[154]

Finally, in the Eucharist, God Himself enters each communicant. If the devil attempts to turn a person toward selfishness and hate, away from the goodness of God and solidarity with his fellow man, the Eucharist is the ultimate antidote. In a talk on the Eucharist, Cardinal Ratzinger speaks of "communion" with Christ as well as with others.

> In my prayers at communion I must, on the one hand, look totally toward Christ, allowing myself to be transformed by him, and, as needed, to be consumed in the fire of his love. But precisely for this reason I must always realize also that he joins me in this way with every other communicant — with the one next to me, whom I may not like very much; but also with those who are far away, whether in Asia, Africa, America, or some other place. By becoming one with them, I must learn to open

[153] Ibid., 193.
[154] Ibid.

myself toward them and to become involved in their situations. This is the test of the authenticity of my love for Christ.[155]

This far-reaching unity usurps the loneliness and idleness in which the evil one thrives.

✳ ✳ ✳

In addition to the spiritual benefits of the liturgy, Joseph Ratzinger emphasizes an active prayer life—especially the Rosary and prayers to the Holy Spirit—in our struggle against evil.

Consider the story of Bartolo Longo, born in the mid-1800s in the Kingdom of the Two Sicilies. While studying at the University of Naples, Longo found himself involved in a satanic cult and was even ordained as a priest in it. What followed was a remarkable conversion to Catholicism. Longo developed a life-long devotion to the Rosary, and as a third-order Dominican, he led efforts to construct the Basilica of Our Lady of the Most Holy Rosary of Pompeii. He was beatified by John Paul II, who visited the shrine in 2003. Benedict visited the shrine in 2008 and Pope Francis in 2015.[156]

Benedict's homily during Mass at this shrine connected Longo's conversion with a reflection on Marian devotion and the fruits of praying the Rosary. Benedict also noted Longo's previous life as a preamble to today:

---

[155] Joseph Ratzinger, "Eucharist—Communio—Solidarity," in *On the Way to Jesus Christ*, 177.

[156] See Elise Harris, "Satanism, Pompeii and the Rosary—a Bizarre Tale Surrounds Francis' Next Trip," Catholic News Agency, March 3, 2015, accessed November 28, 2015, http://www. catholicnewsagency.com/.

The episode of Bartolo Longo's spiritual crisis and conversion appears very relevant today. In fact, in the period of his university studies in Naples, influenced by immanentist and positivist philosophers, he had drifted from the Christian faith. He had become a militant anti-clerical, and even indulged in spiritualistic and superstitious practices. His conversion, with the discovery of God's true Face, contains a very eloquent message for us since, unfortunately, such tendencies are not lacking in our day.[157]

Benedict concluded his sermon certain to make mention of the Rosary's role in the spiritual journey. "The Rosary is a spiritual 'weapon' in the battle against evil, against all violence, for peace in hearts, in families, in society and in the world."[158]

Prayer is vital to the life of the Church. Although Christ's promise to Peter that "the gates of hell would not prevail" against the Church (cf. Matt. 16:18), the promise did not preclude the sins of men from weakening it. As a result of the fading prayer life in many nations, there was now, in the minds of men, a conflict between how the Church was perceived on earth and the supernatural promise she proclaimed through Christ.

For many people today the Church has become the main obstacle to belief. They can no longer see in her anything but the human struggle for power, the petty spectacle of those who, with their claim to administer official

---

[157] Benedict XVI, homily at the Pontifical Shrine of Pompeii, October 19, 2008.
[158] Ibid.

Christianity, seem to stand most in the way of the true spirit of Christianity.[159]

A few years after Professor Ratzinger published these thoughts in *Introduction to Christianity*, Pope Paul VI expressed a disturbing thought that in subsequent decades would come to pass. "*Da qualche fessura sia entrato il fumo di Satana nel tempio di Dio*," he said. "From some fissure the smoke of Satan has entered the temple of God."[160]

How had this happened? Instead of wisdom, understanding, counsel, fortitude, knowledge, piety, and wonder and awe, there was found pride, greed, envy, gluttony, wrath, lust, and sloth. In this smoke of Satan, was emphasis put on the human aspect of the Church, on her societal influence, her institutional prestige, and the characterization of clergy less as priests than as royalty? Had even the lay faithful become too complacent and too perfunctory, complaining about a homily's length or about the musicians or making other excuses to avoid entering the mystery? This smoke of Satan is what Ratzinger railed against in the 2005 Way of the Cross and again in the homily before that year's papal election. It continued in Pope Francis's famous address to the Roman Curia in 2014. His no-nonsense words indicated that the Church's recuperation from her self-inflicted wounds was yet unrealized: "Self-destruction is the most insidious danger. It is the evil which strikes from within; and, as Christ says: 'Every kingdom divided against itself is laid waste' (Luke 11:17)."[161]

---

[159] Ratzinger, *Introduction to Christianity*, 340.

[160] Paul VI, "IX Anniversario Dell'Incoronazione Di Sua Santità," June 29, 1972.

[161] Francis, presentation of the Christmas greetings to the Roman Curia, December 22, 2014.

Ratzinger quotes the book of Revelation in speaking of our day. The Advocate whom Jesus promised would descend upon the faithful, "the adversary of the *diablos*, the 'prosecutor', the slanderer, 'who accuses our brethren day and night before God' (Revelation 12:10)."[162] Ratzinger continues:

> We may say that the Spirit is the Spirit of joy and of the Gospel. One of the basic rules for the discernment of spirits could be formulated as follows: Where joylessness rules and humor dies, we may be certain that the Holy Spirit, the Spirit of Jesus Christ, is not present. Furthermore, joy is a sign of grace. One who is serene from the bottom of his heart, one who has suffered without losing joy, is not far from the God of the Gospel, from the Spirit of God, who is the Spirit of eternal joy.[163]

If joy is not in the lexicon of the evil one, it can only be a force of good — and hope.

---

[162] Ratzinger, *God of Jesus Christ*, 113.
[163] Ibid.

CHAPTER NINE

POPE BENEDICT AND CATHOLIC EDUCATION

When Pope Benedict's resignation went into effect on February 28, 2013, several presidents of U.S. Catholic colleges and universities commented on Benedict's legacy and commitment to Catholic higher education. Nearly all of them commented on the lasting impact of Benedict's April 2008 visit to the United States, particularly his address to Catholic educators at the Catholic University of America (CUA).

Catholic University president John Garvey noted, "[Benedict] encouraged Catholic institutions to embrace their Catholic identity, and to appreciate the unique gifts Catholicism brings to higher education."[164] Two weeks earlier, Garvey had written, "Being Catholic is not simply about what you know, [Benedict] has reminded us time and again, but what you do." Then he

---

[164] Tim Drake, "Symposium: Pope Benedict XVI's Legacy on Catholic Higher Education," Cardinal Newman Society, February 27, 2013, accessed December 1, 2015, http://www.cardinalnewmansociety.org/. See also Garvey's foreword in *A Reason Open to God*.

quoted Benedict: "Far from being just a communication of factual data—'informative'—the loving truth of the Gospel is creative and life-changing—'performative'."[165]

The distinction is central to Benedict XVI's vision that Christianity must be freed from being trapped as an intellectual concept and allowed to become a breathing reality. From the outset of *Spe Salvi*, he emphasized the "performative" nature of the gospel. "That means: the Gospel is not merely a communication of things that can be known—it is one that makes things happen and is life-changing. The dark door of time, of the future, has been thrown open. The one who has hope lives differently; the one who hopes has been granted the gift of a new life."[166]

This idea is also central to his vision of the role of Catholic education. Decades after he graced university halls, the professor-turned-Pontiff observed the effects of social change from the 1960s on the academic world of the new millennium. He was particularly concerned of the growing perception from colleges and universities that freely and joyfully embracing their Catholic identity would cast a pall of orthodoxy. Benedict XVI shattered the notion of the study of Christianity and Catholicism as a solely academic exercise devoid of faith. Distinguishing "performative" from "informative" indicates his desire that educators not only believe in word and action but also embody Christianity in their everyday behavior. In this way, educators, professors, and professional ministers see their position less as a job

---

[165] John Garvey, "Why Benedict Resigned," *National Review*, February 12, 2013, accessed December 1, 2015, http://www.nationalreview.com/.

[166] Benedict XVI, *Spe Salvi*, no. 2.

than as a commitment to a mission. Benedict XVI saw no better place—other than in the family—to offer an array of subjects under a unified umbrella, the pursuit of truth.[167]

Dr. Timothy T. O'Donnell, President of Christendom College in Fort Royal, Virginia, noted:

> Education in truth must guide both the teacher and the student toward objective truth which transcends the particular and the subjective and points the student out of his narrow world towards the universal and absolute. For it is only when the student comes into contact with universal and absolute truth that he will be able to proclaim Christ's message of hope.[168]

In his CUA speech, Benedict addressed how to transform nominally Catholic institutions into bastions of high standards and expectations, where faith and reason form men and women into pillars of hope. "America's brand of secularism" and its influence concerned him. According to this mindset, "faith becomes a passive acceptance that certain things 'out there' are true but without practical relevance for everyday life," he told U.S. bishops a day before his speech on education. "The result is a growing separation of faith from life: living 'as if God did not exist'."[169] Transforming this, Benedict was convinced, would revitalize not

---

[167] See Joseph Ratzinger, "Interpretation—Contemplation—Action: Reflections on the Mission of a Catholic Academy," in *Fundamental Speeches from Five Decades*, 177–199.

[168] Drake, "Symposium."

[169] Benedict XVI, "Responses to the Questions Posed by Bishops," April 16, 2008, q. 1. See also *Pope Benedict in America* (San Francisco: Ignatius Press, 2008) for the complete set of his meetings, homilies, and gatherings in the United States.

only Catholic identity in learning but also the lives of Catholics themselves.

The threat of a relativistic worldview, especially on a college campus rooted in a Catholic identity, lay at the heart of Benedict's concern. The current climate of American education visibly showed its reality.

> Today, a particularly insidious obstacle to the task of educating is the massive presence in our society and culture of that relativism which, recognizing nothing as definitive, leaves the ultimate criterion only the self with its desires. With such a relativistic horizon, therefore, real education is not possible without the light of the truth; sooner or later, every person is in fact condemned to doubting in the goodness of his or her own life and the relationships of which it consists, the validity of his or her commitment to build with others something in common.[170]

Benedict XVI flatly stated in the same speech that "many forces are working to distance us from the faith and from Christian life," molding young minds to perceive with mistrust and disregard the very Faith that provided them with quality education.

And so it is no accident that this former academic chose a university in the United States to deliver — in English — one of his greatest speeches as pope. The speech concerned not just the culture and state of Catholic education but also the persevering and thriving transmission of the Christian way of life. It is nothing short of a manifesto evoking Saint Paul's exhortation: "For necessity is laid upon me. Woe to me if I do not preach

---

[170] Benedict XVI, address to participants in the Ecclesial Diocesan Convention of Rome, June 6, 2015.

the gospel!" (1 Cor. 9:16). The subsequent years since Benedict's 2008 journey have revealed not only an identity crisis in Catholic schools but also campus tumult and student unrest in state and other private schools. This turmoil in higher education is to Benedict yet another systematic representation of a culture struggling with its own narrative—who it is and what it believes. But his dream of a fully realized place of learning reflects his hope for a new kind of humanity. "First and foremost every Catholic educational institution is a place to encounter the living God who in Jesus Christ reveals his transforming love and truth."

More important than the quality of an institution's faculty and administrators, Benedict says, is their "intellectual charity." Educators should believe that their teaching is a "profound responsibility" that is "nothing less than an act of love." With this kind of commitment, high expectations follow. This pursuit of excellence in formation calls for a clear understanding of the purpose and goal of education and even considers its cost. Benedict makes clear that the push "to equate truth with knowledge," which ultimately "denies the foundation of faith and rejects the need for a moral vision," leads not to the formation of the student but to elitism.

Here is another place where relativism can creep in and hamper the individual's view of the transcendent and of his place in the community. "When nothing beyond the individual is recognized as definitive, the ultimate criterion of judgment becomes the self and the satisfaction of the individual's immediate wishes." We see in patterns of college protests across the United States and in those environments that proclaim a tolerance of a spectrum of views that "personal struggles, moral confusion and fragmentation of knowledge" dominate higher education. College is also a tempting time of heightened access for unfettered social experiences in alcohol, drugs, and sexual encounters. When this temperament is viewed as reality, one emerges in a post-academic world with a misaligned compass, "a timidity in the face of the category of the good and an aimless pursuit of novelty as the realization of freedom." It is little wonder that "a lowering of standards occurs." And Benedict is not afraid to again echo the banalization of sexuality in conjunction with this cycle.

> We witness an assumption that every experience is of equal worth and a reluctance to admit imperfection and mistakes. And particularly disturbing is the reduction of the precious and delicate area of education in sexuality to management of "risk", bereft of any reference to the beauty of conjugal love.

In the dictatorship of relativism, truth is concealed by a skewed ideology of toleration, an emphasis on feelings and perceptions and a false sense that truth cannot be known—or that there is no truth altogether. Crisis, then, is the only reliable recurrence. Benedict noted it as such. "The contemporary 'crisis of truth' is rooted in a 'crisis of faith'."

In an educational milieu that breathes positivity and joy with expectations that prompt students to strive for their best, however, we would find Joseph Ratzinger's path toward truth, beauty, and goodness. We would find encounter, metanoia, and joy in endless possibilities. Therefore, in laying out the "complex phenomenon" of the hesitation in taking the step toward a commitment to God, Benedict XVI saves his most penetrating questions for the educators themselves. But he freely admits that he himself "ponders" this very phenomenon "continually," an educator himself.

It is a question of conviction—do we really believe that only in the mystery of the Word made flesh does the mystery of man truly become clear? Are we ready to commit our entire self—intellect and will, mind and heart—to God? Do we accept the truth Christ reveals? Is the faith tangible in our universities and schools? Is it given fervent expression liturgically, sacramentally, through prayer, acts of charity, a concern for justice, and respect for God's creation?[171]

Such questions might be expected from a pope, but they go to the heart of the tension in Catholic education in the United States. In 1967, twenty-six North American university presidents and officials crafted what became known as the Land O' Lakes Statement during a convention in Land O' Lakes, Wisconsin. It was held at a conference center owned by the University of Notre Dame and hosted by its president at the time, Theodore M. Hesburgh, C.S.C.[172]

The statement's purpose was effectively to "declare independence from all authority outside of the institution itself, including the Catholic Church."[173] Although only nine univer-

---

[171] Benedict XVI, address during meeting with Catholic educators, April 17, 2008. See also "Pope Benedict XVI Speech," YouTube video, 25:34, posted by "CatholicUniversity," June 12, 2013, https://www.youtube.com/watch?v=8_N7UlgZjHg.

[172] See David J. O'Brien, "The Land O'Lakes Statement," *Boston College Magazine* (Winter 1998), http://www.bc.edu/.

[173] CNS Staff, Adam Wilson, "Timeline and Background of Ex Corde Ecclesiae," Cardinal Newman Society, August 15, 2010, accessed December 4, 2015, http://www.cardinalnewmansociety.org/.

sities signed the Land O'Lakes Statement, it served as a future reference for other Catholic institutions to claim they had the right to remain independent while retaining their Catholic identity.[174] It also was seen as a launching point for "an era of theological dissent, moral confusion, unfamiliarity with the Catholic intellectual tradition, and rejection of the authority of the Vatican and bishops over Catholic doctrine, practice and identity."[175]

Spurred by this development, more than twenty years later John Paul II crafted "a sort of 'magna carta', enriched by the long and fruitful experience of the Church in the realm of Universities and open to the promise of future achievements that will require courageous creativity and rigorous fidelity."[176] This document, *Ex Corde Ecclesiae*, "was the Church's first official document defining a Catholic college."[177] It was not a direct response to the Land O' Lakes Statement; it makes no mention of it. Rather, John Paul II praised the role of universities:

> They give me a well-founded hope for a new flowering of Christian culture in the rich and varied context of our changing times, which certainly face serious challenges but which also bear so much promise under the action of the Spirit of truth and of love.[178]

---

[174] See Peter Steinfels, "Catholic Identity: Emerging Consensus," *Occasional Papers on Catholic Higher Education* (November 1995): 11–19.

[175] Wilson, "Timeline."

[176] John Paul II, *Ex Corde Ecclesiae* (Apostolic Constitution on Catholic Universities), August 15, 1990, no. 8.

[177] Wilson, "Timeline."

[178] John Paul II, *Ex Corde Ecclesiae*, no. 2.

Although not intentionally, Land O' Lakes and *Ex Corde Ecclesiae* epitomize the two poles of an institution's adherence to its Catholic identity. "Because of the inner disharmony between the two, to choose one is to reject the other."[179]

Such was the landscape of mission and identity in Catholic education when Benedict took the stage at Catholic University. He found that universities were hesitant to implement the teachings of *Ex Corde Ecclesiae*. He also noted unenthusiastic responses to a commitment to a life of faith on the part of institutions and individuals.

This dovetailed with *will* and *freedom*, two ideas central to a humanity's understanding of itself, which Benedict included in his address.

Again, we see why fostering personal intimacy with Jesus Christ and communal witness to his loving truth is indispensable in Catholic institutions of learning. Yet we all know, and observe with concern, the difficulty or reluctance many people have today in entrusting themselves to God. It is a complex phenomenon and one which I ponder continually. While we have sought diligently to engage the intellect of our young, perhaps we have neglected the will. Subsequently, we observe, with distress, the notion of freedom being distorted. Freedom is not an opting out. It is an opting in — a participation in Being itself. Hence authentic freedom can never be attained by turning away from God.[180]

---

[179] Kevin M. Clarke, "Benedict XVI's Call to 'Intellectual Charity'," *Zenit*, February 11, 2011, accessed December 4, 2015, http://www.zenit.org/.

[180] Benedict XVI, meeting with Catholic educators.

✳ ✳ ✳

A rather poignant precursor to the visit to Catholic University was the visit that didn't happen—to Rome's Sapienza University, where Benedict was scheduled to speak on January 17, 2008. The Vatican announced the cancellation of his visit two days before. The decision to withdraw was a result of a protest at La Sapienza from "a handful of professors, 67 out of a total of 4,500, and a few dozen students, out of a total of 135,000" (La Sapienza has the largest university enrollment in Europe).[181] These protestors took issue with what they claimed to be Benedict XVI's "hostility" to science and reason and said that he should speak only of spiritual matters. Ultimately, these 67 disregarded Joseph Ratzinger's lifetime of merging faith and reason and took aim at his purported defense of the Church's seventeenth-century treatment of Galileo (particularly a misinterpreted line from a 1990 conference at La Sapienza).[182]

On January 16, the rector of La Sapienza, Renato Guarino, received a letter from the Vatican secretary of state: "Since at the initiative of a decidedly minority group of professors and students, the conditions for a dignified and peaceful welcome were lacking, it has been judged prudent to delay the scheduled visit in order to remove any pretext for demonstrations that would have been unpleasant for all." But rather than letting the

---

[181] Sandro Magister, "The University of Rome Closes Its Doors to the Pope. Here's the Lesson They Didn't Want to Hear," Chiesa, January 17, 2008, accessed December 6, 2015, http://chiesa.espresso.repubblica.it/articolo/186421?eng=y.

[182] Paolo Centofanti, "Defending the Pope and Paying the Price," Zenit, January 23, 2008, accessed December 6, 2015, http://www.zenit.org/.

cancellation be the last word, the Vatican published Benedict's planned speech in *L'Osservatore Romano* on January 16. Earlier that day, students from La Sapienza's Communion and Liberation movement attended Benedict's general audience as a show of support for the Pope, who spoke on Saint Augustine. "'So there are three places where the pope cannot go: Moscow, Beijing, and the university of Rome,' commented one of the young people present at the audience. 'If Benedict does not go to La Sapienza, La Sapienza comes to Benedict', read one of the banners."[183]

To the dismay of the dissenters, a scan of the speech's text reveals "reason" referenced more than twenty-five times. Anticipating the discord of a Roman Pontiff speaking on the very issue of reason, even using it as a starting point for his reflections on questions such as, *What is reason? What is the university? What is its task?*, Benedict even proposed the questions, *What is the nature and mission of the Papacy?* and *What can and should the Pope say at a meeting with the university in his city?*[184] That Benedict XVI was prevented from pondering these questions in a public forum at an institution of higher learning foreshadowed the tenuous position of freedom of speech in the public sphere.

A year and a half after the fallout at La Sapienza, at a meeting with academics in the Czech Republic, Benedict found an opportunity to question the foundation for this rising mentality in higher education:

---

[183] "University Students Greet the Pope with Chants of 'Freedom, Freedom!'" Asianews.it, January 16, 2008, accessed December 7, 2015, http://www.asianews.it/index.php?l=en&art=11263& size=A.

[184] Benedict XVI, lecture at the University of Rome "La Sapienza," January 17, 2008.

The relativism that ensues provides a dense camouflage behind which new threats to the autonomy of academic institutions can lurk. While the period of interference from political totalitarianism has passed, is it not the case that frequently, across the globe, the exercise of reason and academic research are—subtly and not so subtly—constrained to bow to the pressures of ideological interest groups and the lure of short-term utilitarian or pragmatic goals? What will happen if our culture builds itself only on fashionable arguments, with little reference to a genuine historical intellectual tradition, or on the viewpoints that are most vociferously promoted and most heavily funded? What will happen if in its anxiety to preserve a radical secularism, it detaches itself from its life-giving roots? Our societies will not become more reasonable or tolerant or adaptable but rather more brittle and less inclusive, and they will increasingly struggle to recognize what is true, noble and good.[185]

Engaging the students' will and intellect with authentic witness of word and action from educators would naturally lead to the pursuit of truth. Joseph Ratzinger was convinced of this, and it was his lasting message concerning Catholic education.

The rejection by the La Sapienza protestors that prohibited Benedict XVI from speaking there crystallized the fundamental misreading of him that continues to prevent acknowledgment of his contribution. Instead many consider him the doctrinal watchdog, the physical embodiment of the pall of orthodoxy,

---

[185] Benedict XVI, address at a meeting with members of the academic community, September 27, 2009.

the blockade against personal autonomy that threatens to shut him out of public discovery.

We have considered Benedict's achievements through concepts and ideas. But here we quote from a passionate passage about his concern for the misreading that not so much damaged his reputation as hindered true conversion to the real faith of Jesus Christ. This was the view of Catholicism that prevented generations from pursuing it, a "religion" wrapped in its own legalism and royalty, both saccharine and condemnatory, hypocritical and unmerciful — and thus altogether un-Christian. And Joseph Ratzinger was the public face of it, as La Sapienza attested and as the reaction after Regensburg revealed. Who would want to be a member of that faith? Ratzinger saw this view as disastrous:

> I was disturbed by the idea that faith was a virtually intolerable burden, something only the really strong could shoulder. Perhaps it would be going too far to call faith a punishment, but it certainly posed extremely high demands that were difficult to satisfy. In other words, faith made salvation harder, not easier. One should therefore rejoice if the obligation to believe is not imposed upon one, since that would mean being bowed down by the yoke of the morality of the Catholic Church.[186]

In this passage, Cardinal Ratzinger speaks about his discussion regarding conscience with a colleague and the notion that a good conscience should be free of "the burden of faith and its moral obligations." It is an impression many have held throughout time, but more so today, when spirituality remains vibrant, but

---

[186] Joseph Ratzinger, "If You Want Peace ..." in *Values in a Time of Upheaval* (San Francisco: Ignatius Press, 2006), 77–78.

religious association is declining. "If such an idea of faith were to spread, it would have fatal consequences," Ratzinger writes. "I am convinced that the traumatic aversion that many people feel *toward* what they regard as '*preconciliar*' *Catholicism* has its roots in their *encounter with* this kind of *faith, which was nothing more than a burden.*"[187] One clearly sees the unbridled energy in the writing, similar to his tone after the Second Vatican Council when upheaval dominated parish life with waves of people exiting churches, simply because, as he states here, the faith wasn't correctly exemplified.

> Truth would not be something that sets us free, but something from which we need to be set free.... Would it not actually be better to spare [others] from coming to the faith? It is obvious that ideas of this kind have paralyzed the willingness on the part of Christians in recent decades to engage in evangelization, and this is logical: one who experiences faith as a heavy load, as an exacting moral challenge, will not want to invite others to believe. One will prefer to leave them in the supposed freedom of their good conscience.[188]

The crisis in education today, marked by protests clamoring for change, is itself a crisis. In protesting, an invaluable education is being overlooked or downright ignored. The campuses may be brimming, but the classrooms are empty. As much as this is true at a university, so too is culture itself dimming in intellectual and moral reach.

---

[187] Ibid., 78.
[188] Ibid.

CHAPTER TEN

THE BENEDICTINE
SPRING

*Benedict does not say, "Believe what I say." Rather
he says, "This is the argument as I understand it."*

—James Schall, *The Regensburg Lecture*

When fire was set to the Reichstag building on February 27,
1933, Joseph Aloisius Ratzinger was five years old. Nearly eighty
years after the burning put in motion the rise of Adolf Hitler,
the same Joseph Ratzinger, the first German pope in almost 950
years, appeared before parliamentary representatives of the Fed-
eral Republic of Germany, including Chancellor Angela Merkel
and President Christian Wulff. Even though Benedict XVI had
been invited by the German government to deliver an address,
throngs of protestors crowded Berlin's streets outsides. Some held
signs, such as one featuring the *Ghostbusters* logo, the befuddled
ghost wearing a bishop's miter and pectoral cross with the website
domain "notwelcome.de" underneath it. "Separation of church
and state!" claimed a woman holding the "Not welcome" sign.
"I know they made some kind of deal because the Pope is the

head of Vatican state, but I think this is cheating, that's not a right thing to do."[189]

Clearly, the spirit of the sixty-seven La Sapienza objectors in 2008 carried over to the Pope's homeland more than three years later. To those vehemently opposed to whatever the Bishop of Rome says or wherever he goes, one thing is certain: Joseph Ratzinger is a friend of neither science nor reason. He is either dismissive or authoritarian or both, and he has no business speaking of matters of law and politics. (The title of his presentation at the *Bundestag* was "The Listening Heart: Reflections on the Foundations of Law.") The uproar after Regensburg in September 2006 seemed to have closed the book on any positive outlook on Benedict XVI for the remainder of his papacy. Antipathy was the lingering consensus.

The protests outside the Reichstag building, the heated opposition that threatened his arrival to the United Kingdom a year earlier, the disgruntlement at La Sapienza, and the mayhem after Regensburg revealed the polarization of a message increasingly at odds with the cultural path of the twenty-first century, or an unwillingness to reflect on the message altogether, as well as a collective display of relativism.

Nazi ideology had left a diabolical legacy that Joseph Ratzinger would often fight against. While he would condemn anything that might suggest a movement toward totalitarianism, he also saw the dangers in modern notions that equated freedom with positivism. Seeing such notions, Pope Benedict addressed the modern political confusion in his Reichstag lecture:

[189] "Pope Benedict XVI Addresses German Parliament; Thousands Protest," YouTube video, 2:55–3:09, posted by "AP Archive," July 30, 2015, https://www.youtube.com/watch?v= q3aOaZ6iC4Q.

There are concerted efforts to recognize only positivism as a common culture and a common basis for law-making, reducing all the other insights and values of our culture to the level of subculture, with the result that Europe vis-à-vis other world cultures is left in a state of culturelessness and at the same time extremist and radical movements emerge to fill the vacuum.[190]

Although the role of the Pope in modern times is primarily one of spiritual guidance, he must not ignore the tangible aspects of life and disregard the Catholic who must immerse himself in the world as a citizen and person of faith. Pope Benedict fostered a path toward living truthfully as a dedicated Christian who is loyal to both God and Caesar. This is a fact that should be cherished rather than protested.

Benedict's Reichstag speech continued an interesting pattern that occurred over his pontificate: the significance of his September speeches. In nearly every September of his pontificate, he delivered a major international address about fundamental facets of life concerning the present state of affairs and the context of its development: at Regensburg in 2006, at the Collège des Bernardins in Paris in 2008, at Prague Castle in 2009, at Westminster Hall in 2010, in Berlin in 2011, and finally, at the Baabda Presidential Palace in Beirut, during his final international journey in September 2012. The political, social, and cultural impact of such discourses was not lost on Professor Marc D. Guerra, who

---

[190] Benedict XVI, "The Listening Heart: Reflections on the Foundations of Law," address at the Reichstag building, Berlin, September 22, 2011.

edited these speeches in the book *Liberating Logos*. "Besides providing a model of what an intellectually engaged, thoughtful, and faithful 'Catholic mind' looks like to the world, he also shows those of us in the world of Catholic higher education what this kind of mind looks like," Guerra noted.[191]

Although we have seen how great cultural incidents directly affected Ratzinger's life and career, the acceleration of seismic events in the twenty-first century involved not only large communities and countries but also Benedict XVI's papacy and his own assessment of his leadership. In the few years prior to his ascendancy in 2005, violent extremism involved the entire planet, sparked by the catastrophe of September 11, 2001, and the ensuing War on Terror. Thanks to the investigative journalism of the *Boston Globe* the sexual-abuse scandal that began an avalanche in the United States was exposed. The failing health of John Paul II hampered effective responses to both, sometimes resulting in harsh criticism.[192]

While taking on more responsibilities as prefect for the Congregation of the Doctrine of the Faith, Cardinal Ratzinger frequently lent his personal insights to the unfolding of the world as he saw it throughout Italy and Europe in numerous speeches.[193] John Paul occasionally summoned the energy to combat what he saw as the threats of the day, but he realized that in the third

---

[191] Justin Petrisek, "Pope Benedict's Vision Key to Survival of Catholic Colleges, Says Author," *Catholic Education Daily*, April 8, 2015, accessed December 16, 2015, http://www.cardinalnewmansociety.org/CatholicEducationDaily/.

[192] See John Cornwell, *The Pontiff in Winter: Triumph and Conflict in the Reign of John Paul II* (New York: Doubleday, 2004).

[193] Joseph Ratzinger, *Christianity and the Crisis of Cultures*. See also *Dialectics of Secularization* (San Francisco: Ignatius Press, 2007).

millennium—which he exuberantly saw as a symbolic time of conversion to God—a new world was dawning, and a clear, calm voice was needed to help make sense of the rising tide of uncertainty.[194]

Such was the fate that befell Joseph Ratzinger. For him to ignore the consequences of technological advancement, bioethical issues, extremism, institutional corruption, financial instability, political unrest, and social, psychological, and religious decline would be a disservice to society. If there was anyone in authority who was able to speak on such matters with knowledge and clarity, it was Joseph Ratzinger. Between his intellectual capability and his career experiences, he found himself situated at precisely the best angle to counter all the force that moral relativism could garner.

The opportunities to speak out against injustices sometimes took him into unwelcome arenas. He was an icon of truth in the lion's den, even in his own homeland. On the morning of September 12, 2006, Benedict XVI celebrated the Eucharist before a huge crowd gathered on Islinger Field near Regensburg, Germany. In his customary style of employing rhetorical questions, the pontiff asked his native people: "What do we actually believe? What does it mean to have faith? Is it still something possible in the modern world?"[195] Always concerning himself

---

[194] "'NO TO WAR!' War Is Not Always Inevitable" John Paul II exclaimed at the outset of 2003, two months before the launch of Operation Iraqi Freedom. John Paul II, address to the Diplomatic Corps, January 13, 2003, no. 4. See also "Turbulence of History: 2001–2002" in George Weigel, *The End and the Beginning*.

[195] Benedict XVI, homily during Mass in Regensburg, September 12, 2006.

with the root of things, Benedict revealed an insight in this homily that prefigured the Regensburg address he would give later that day.

> We believe in God. But what God? Certainly we believe in the God who is Creator Spirit, creative Reason, the source of everything that exists, including ourselves. This creative Reason is Goodness, it is Love. It has a face. God does not leave us groping in the dark.... Today, when we have learned to recognize the pathologies and the life-threatening diseases associated with religion and reason, and the ways that God's image can be destroyed by hatred and fanaticism, it is important to state clearly the God in whom we believe, and to proclaim confidently that this God has a human face. Only this can free us from being afraid of God—which is ultimately at the root of modern atheism.[196]

We have already considered political and social examples of how Benedict concerned himself with pressing for dialogue and action to reach the root of problems that, more often than not, are sidestepped so that cursory issues instead become the focus. As Father Schall detailed in his book-length study of the Regensburg speech, and as we have seen throughout our journey, the perception of Benedict as forcing religion upon free peoples is anything but true. He simply proposes that we counter humility with pride, and selflessness with valuing other human life. He shows us that the seeker of goodwill inevitably will encounter the Person of Jesus Christ. In doing so, Joseph Ratzinger firmly believed a transformation would occur in which justice, truth,

---

[196] Ibid.

and peace would emerge and a pathway to salvation would be made clear.

> It is precisely man's forgetfulness of God, and his failure to give him glory, which gives rise to violence.... The consequences of forgetfulness of God cannot be separated from those resulting from ignorance of his true countenance, the root of a baneful religious fanaticism. As I have often observed, this is a falsification of religion itself, since religion aims instead at reconciling men and women with God, at illuminating and purifying consciences, and at making it clear that each human being is the image of the Creator.[197]

With increasing access to science and technology, and a lack of ethical foundations to guide their use, the demand for progress frequently distorts our notions of freedom, reason, and governance. Then, because even a faint notion of progress has a great influence on the populace, the very foundations of democratic rule begin to crumble. Opposing these influences calls for more than a cry from the conservative heart for simpler times.

> The continued course of technological development will ensure that the belief in progress does not die out and thereby that political messianism, too, remains alive in changing forms.... The consequences of the destruction of ethical foundations are in fact becoming dramatically visible today in the epidemic spread of a civilization of death.

---

[197] Benedict XVI, address to the members of the Diplomatic Corps accredited to the Holy See," January 7, 2013.

Here, Cardinal Ratzinger (writing in 1990) cites specific situations that result from such destruction:

> The countries that live off the production of drugs are linked to those who consume them by a highway of death that becomes wider and wider and needs less and less to conceal itself. Terrorism needs no ideological excuse today; it reveals itself nakedly as the self-evident fact of violence that justifies itself through its successes. Robber bands challenge the state and can establish themselves as a kind of counterstate.[198]

He is also quite aware that revealing such realities can only raise awareness. Charting a course for renewal is the seemingly insurmountable challenge. Given the number of major figures in politics and society who heard the great cultural speeches of Benedict XVI, the awareness aspect seems obvious. "Freedom is very demanding," he acknowledges. "It does not keep itself alive, and it ceases to exist precisely when it attempts to be boundless." Jesus tells us, "When the unclean spirit has gone out of a man, he passes through waterless places seeking rest, but he finds none. Then he says, 'I will return to my house from which I came.' And when he comes he finds it empty, swept, and put in order. Then he goes and brings with him seven other spirits more evil than himself, and they enter and dwell there" (Matt. 12:43–45).

History shows again and again the truth of Jesus' image. The loss of a hitherto life-supporting ideology can very easily result in nihilism, and that would truly be the reign of the seven worse spirits. But who could ignore the

---

[198] Ratzinger, *Turning Point*, 132–133.

growing tendency to nihilism on the part of the relativism to which we are all exposed today?[199]

"May you have a strong foundation," Bob Dylan sings in "Forever Young," "when the winds of changes shift." Joseph Ratzinger is demanding mankind to determine what exactly that strong foundation is and whether the will exists to nurture it. He reminds us that in a culture that views science as infallible, and where much good has undoubtedly been attained, left unchecked, "science can also serve inhumanity! Here we may recall the weapons of mass destruction, medical experiments on human beings, or the treatment of a person merely as a store of usable organs. It must be clear that science too is subject to moral criteria."[200]

Yet how does a civilization serious about investment in the well-being and future of its people construct tangible foundations? Again, the man accused of being an enemy of reason and all things rational cites reason — "right reason" (*ratio recta*) — as the basis. The collapse of right reason, Ratzinger believes, "signifies a crisis of political reason, which is a crisis of politics as such."

All who bear responsibility for peace and justice in the world — and in the last analysis, that means all of us — have the urgent task of working to overcome this state of affairs. This endeavor is by no means hopeless, since reason itself will always make its voice heard against the abuse of power and one-sided partisanship.[201]

Right reason does not necessarily mean that the opinion of the majority rules. In "Political Visions and Political Praxis,"

---

[199] Ibid., 152.
[200] Ratzinger, "Political Visions and Political Praxis," in *Values*, 26.
[201] Ibid., 27.

Cardinal Ratzinger set forth many ideas on how to build a strong foundation and of checks and balance in government. He speaks of "the limitations of the principle of consensus" and suggests as an example the Ten Commandments. Insofar as faith is seen in the public sphere as a dangerous ideology, a retreat from rationality, an exclusive means to salvation, it will always be a "religion" of dogmas, doctrines, and rules and thus something that must be privatized (that is, irrelevant).

What Joseph Ratzinger offers again and again, particularly in works concerning political structures with the influence to shape opinions and lives, is a natural just order, for we have seen the consequences of unadulterated reason, which itself becomes a totalitarian regime. "Must we not therefore say that it is reason that needs a guardian?"[202]

How, then, can a claim be made toward a foundation rooted in faith that affects peoples of diverse cultures and beliefs without arrogantly undermining those personal values? Is it even possible? "The obligation to subject ourselves not just to follow our own wishes can amount to a great school in being human and can make man capable of recognizing and appreciating truth."

The will to let oneself be purified by the truth is essential. The capacity to renounce oneself, a greater inner openness, the discipline to withdraw ourselves from noise and all that presses on our attention, should once more be for all of us goals that we recognize as being among

---

[202] Ratzinger, "The Moral Foundations of a Free State," in *Values in a Time of Upheaval*, 37.

our priorities. Let us be honest about it: today there is a hypertrophy of the outer man, and his inner strength has been alarmingly weakened.[203]

All of these concepts, which can quickly turn into abstracts, are meaningless without the foundation for a just society: charity. *Caritas in Veritate*, Benedict XVI's final completed encyclical from 2009, illustrates this theme for a time upended by financial instability, rising unemployment, unprecedented growth in terror-related incidents, and family and community fragmentation. While focusing on Christian charity and its place in the world, *Caritas in Veritate* attempts a sweeping study of the major social issues of the early twenty-first century. It does so through a prism of economic justice and of a growing urgency and prevalence of human ecology in the political sphere and in personal lifestyles.

The English translation of the letter's title, "Charity in Truth," suggests the heart of Benedict's proposal. "A Christianity of charity without truth would be more or less interchangeable with a pool of good sentiments, helpful for social cohesion, but of little relevance," he writes. "In other words, there would be no longer any real place for God in the world."[204]

In *Caritas in Veritate* Benedict XVI connects the social crises unfolding in the midst of unrivaled accumulation of wealth, technological expansion, and globalization with a Church struggling to convey her message to many parts of the world. This was foreseen by Peter Seewald a few years earlier as he surveyed the modern European landscape threatening to spread across

---

[203] *Truth and Tolerance*, 159.
[204] Benedict XVI, *Caritas in Veritate*, no. 4.

the globe: "The religious decline of a people is usually followed by a decline in its intellectual and economic productivity."[205] As unpopular as it made popes and the Church they guided, life seen through the lens of the face of Jesus Christ and the creative reason of the triune God awakens an openness to all life, an openness to the natural world in which all life is graced. To push against it in various capacities leads to a cycle that can be only effectively termed a "culture of death."[206]

> The book of nature is one and indivisible: it takes in not only the environment but also life, sexuality, marriage, the family, social relations: in a word, integral human development. Our duties towards the environment are linked to our duties towards the human person, considered in himself and in relation to others. It would be wrong to uphold one set of duties while trampling on the other. Herein lies a grave contradiction in our mentality and practice today: one which demeans the person, disrupts the environment and damages society.[207]

If it is agreed that disorder lurks amid all progress and achievements, how do we reorient our priorities? "How much error and folly, greed, violence, and falsehood, how much crime," Romano Guardini wrote in his book on virtues. "All this exists in spite of science, technology, and welfare—or rather, together with it, mixed with it, inextricably confused."

[205] Peter Seewald, *Benedict XVI: Servant of Truth* (San Francisco: Ignatius Press, 2006), 135.
[206] See John Paul II, *Evangelium Vitae* (The Gospel of Life), March 25, 1995. "Culture of death" is cited twelve times.
[207] Benedict XVI, *Caritas in Veritate*, no. 51.

It exists even in religion, in men's ideas of the divine, their relations with it, and their defense of it. Modern man is inclined simply to accept everything that happens. He arranges one thing next to the other, declares everything to be necessary, and calls the whole "history." But he who has learned to distinguish, to call the true, true and the false, false, the right, right and the wrong, wrong, cannot do this and must be frightened to see how man deals with the world.[208]

In the fifth chapter of *Caritas in Veritate*, "The Cooperation of the Human Family," Benedict XVI explains how theological and secular concerns are intertwined, showing how solidarity within the family leads to solidarity within the larger civilization, and ultimately to unity with God. "*In the light of the revealed mystery of the Trinity*, we understand that true openness does not mean loss of individual identity but profound interpenetration. This also emerges from the common human experiences of love and truth."[209]

Respect for life, the heart of human ecology, by its nature expresses a hope in humanity: that all life by its very existence is good. To believe in a Giver of life is a recognition of not only man's creatureliness but also his greatness. Rooted in God's footprint as man, in Jesus, the believer can only promote the justice of all human life and share in the joy of being great, of being unique, and cherished. The Church's social teaching, her commitment to family structure, her call for political, economic, and social justice, and even in her theology and

---

[208] Romano Guardini, *Learning the Virtues That Lead You to God* (Manchester, NH: Sophia Institute Press, 1998), 36.

[209] Benedict XVI, *Caritas in Veritate*, no. 54.

understanding of revelation are all oriented toward enabling each life to receive the opportunity to encounter the greatness that lies within. "Christ shows God to us, and thus the true greatness of man."[210]

---

[210] Benedict XVI, address to the German pilgrims in Rome for the inauguration ceremony of the pontificate, April 25, 2005.

CHAPTER ELEVEN

RESIGNED TO JOY

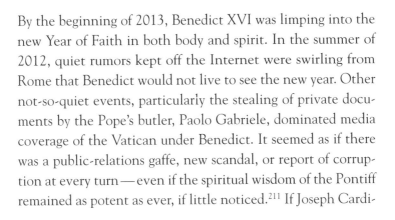

By the beginning of 2013, Benedict XVI was limping into the new Year of Faith in both body and spirit. In the summer of 2012, quiet rumors kept off the Internet were swirling from Rome that Benedict would not live to see the new year. Other not-so-quiet events, particularly the stealing of private documents by the Pope's butler, Paolo Gabriele, dominated media coverage of the Vatican under Benedict. It seemed as if there was a public-relations gaffe, new scandal, or report of corruption at every turn — even if the spiritual wisdom of the Pontiff remained as potent as ever, if little noticed.[211] If Joseph Cardi-

---

[211] Emer McCarthy, "Papal Visit and Christmas Pardon for Paolo Gabriele," *Vatican Radio*, December 22, 2015, http://www.news.va/en/news/papal-visit-and-christmas-pardon-for-paolo-gabriel. The Italian journalist, Gianluggi Nuzzi, published the documents in *Ratzinger Was Afraid*. Three years later, he published *Merchants in the Temple: Inside Pope Francis's Secret Battle against Corruption in the Vatican*, shortly before coming under investigation for the publication of stolen documents, a felony under Vatican law revised by Pope Francis. See Inés San Martín, "Journalists Who Published Leaks Refuse Vatican Interrogation," *Crux*, November 17, 2015, accessed December 14, 2015,

nal Ratzinger foresaw a movement toward the dictatorship of relativism in April 2005, it revealed its presence in one sordid story after another at the end of the Benedictine papacy. And even afterward, revelations surfaced of a faction called the St. Gallen "Mafia" who attempted to dissuade voting cardinals from electing the cardinal-prefect Joseph Ratzinger in 2005.[212]

The contents of Benedict's personal correspondence that Paolo Gabriele leaked contained "tales of rivalry and betrayal, and allegations of corruption and systemic dysfunction that infused the inner workings of the Holy See."[213] At the center of the documents was Archbishop Carlo Maria Viganò, appointed by Benedict XVI "to enact a series of reforms within the Vatican." *The Washington Post* reported, "In one missive, Viganò wrote to [then–Vatican Secretary of State Cardinal] Bertone accusing him of getting in the way of the pope's reform mission."[214]

To Peter Seewald, Benedict was at this stage a shadow of the "freshness of youth" the German writer noted so long ago. "I had never seen him so exhausted," Seewald observed. "His hearing had gone down, he was blind in the left eye, his body had

---

http://www.cruxnow.com/church/2015/11/17/journalist-who-published-leaked-documents-refuses-vatican-interrogation/.

[212] Edward Pentin, "Cardinal Daneels' Biographers Retract Comments on St. Gallen Group," *National Catholic Register*, September 26, 2015, accessed December 14, 2015, http://www.ncregister.com/blog/edward-pentin/st.-gallen-group-not-a-lobby-group-say-authors.

[213] Jason Horowitz, "Pope Benedict XVI's Leaked Documents Show Fractured Vatican Full of Rivalries," *Washington Post*, February 16, 2013, accessed December 14, 2015, https://www.washingtonpost.com/.

[214] Ibid.

grown thinner."[215] But, Seewald believed VatiLeaks—as it came to be known—was less a motive for resignation than a chance for the reform Pope Ratzinger yearned to be accomplished. "It was very important for the Pope that the VatiLeaks exposure would ensure an independent judiciary in the Vatican," Seewald commented.[216]

Reading the reports and attempting to draw a conclusion from the chaos might understandably detour a serious seeker who is inclined to the pursuit of God and truth to dismiss this Vatican's Byzantine web as a tainted political machination. It might even cast it as the representative not of the Church built on the rock of Peter but of the forces of darkness it seeks to crush. An online search quickly satisfies that angle. The movements undermining Benedict's ministry all indicated the presence of ambition, power, and scheming. We see an apparent unwillingness to embrace the message that Joseph Ratzinger sought to inject into a new era of Catholicism. Competing forces hindered him from fully realizing his vision—a new way for a new time to meet Christ once again. That such a force would lurk within the halls the Pope himself graced only punctuates the truth from a passage in Isaiah:

> Listen carefully, but you shall not understand!
> Look intently, but you shall know nothing!
> You are to make the heart of this people sluggish,
>   to dull their ears and close their eyes;

[215] Catherine Harmon, "Seewald: Vatileaks Didn't Influence Benedict's Decision to Resign," *Catholic World Report*, February 19, 2013, accessed December 14, 2015, http://www.catholicworld report.com/.

[216] Ibid.

Else their eyes will see, their ears hear, their heart
understand, and they will turn and be healed.
(Isa. 6:9–10, NABRE)

As the *Washington Post's* Jason Horowitz puts it, VatiLeaks
"exposed the church bureaucracy's entrenched opposition to
Benedict's fledgling effort to carve out a legacy as a reformer
against the backdrop of a global child sex abuse scandal and
the continued dwindling of his flock."[217] The affair threatened
to derail everything Joseph Ratzinger worked to accomplish
over a lifetime of service. That it confirmed everything he fore-
warned yielded little consolation. Somehow, though, his vision
remained joyfully optimistic. It was more "Adeste Fidelis" than
"Dies Irae," as if the secret to "keeping one's gaze" on God is
nothing more than facing the travails of life with the attitude of
the adoring shepherds at Bethlehem. "Keeping one's gaze freely
fixed upon God," he wrote, "in order to receive from him the
criterion of right action and the capacity for it—that is what
matters."[218]

As Benedict XVI's matter-of-fact intention to resign occurred
on the World Day of the Sick, early speculation looked to Benedict's frail health as the main indicator for resignation.

His departure during the Year of Faith and during Lent was
also significant. In his final public homily as Benedict XVI, Ash
Wednesday 2013, he reflected on a line from that day's first
reading from the Book of Joel:

---

[217] Jason Horowitz, "Pope Benedict's Leaked Documents Show
Fractured Vatican Full of Rivalries," *Washington Post*, February
16, 2013.

[218] Benedict XVI, *Jesus of Nazareth: Holy Week*, 288.

Finally, the prophet considers the prayer of the priests, who turn to God with tears, saying: "Do not make your heritage a mockery, a byword among the nations." ... This prayer makes us think of the importance of the witness of Christian faith and life given by each of us and our communities for showing the face of the Church, and how that face is sometimes disfigured. I think in particular of sins against the unity of the Church, and divisions within the body of the Church.[219]

Pope Benedict consistently avoided making direct and particular rebukes. Here, though, the implication toward the swirling drama around him is masterfully conveyed amid the larger sins that divide the Church. He laments the possible saints who may have been made if not for the political maneuvering they witness within the Church.

In his final Sunday Angelus a few days later, Benedict highlighted the primacy of prayer in the life of the Christian. This would be his primary responsibility in his retirement phase. There would not be a return of the globetrotting cardinal delivering epic speeches on faith and culture, or a new outpouring of writings authored by Joseph Ratzinger. There would be an example of the fundamental Christian practice of communication with God. The departure from the Vatican on February 28, 2013 would be the last time Benedict XVI would be subject to media scrutiny as the reigning Pontiff. In his appearances as Pope emeritus, he made certain he was only a sideline participant. But in the dramatic exodus in a helicopter over the Roman landscape,

---

[219] Benedict XVI, Ash Wednesday homily, February 13, 2013, Vatican basilica.

first from Vatican City then to Castel Gandolfo, brilliantly shot by the Vatican Television Center, wonder and awe surrounded the ancient Church so besieged by attempts to tear down and demolish the beauty, truth, and goodness she has sustained over the millennia.[220]

At that last Angelus in Castel Gandolfo, Benedict correlated the Gospel reading for the Second Sunday of Lent. It was on the Transfiguration, a fitting concluding reading for the Pope who yearned for the rediscovery of the transfigured human face of God. Benedict clarified that prayer does not mean isolation and abandonment: "Prayer leads back to the journey and to action"—even if the journey seems over and action a surrender to forces too powerful to combat.[221]

Joseph Ratzinger has his eyes set on a further aim. He can now only pray that others are inspired to follow.

---

[220] "Pope's Departure from the Vatican—2013-02-28," YouTube video, 1:22:06, posted by "EWTN," February 28, 2013, https:// www.youtube.com/watch?v=NvtBYIXc7YY.

[221] Benedict XVI, Angelus, February 24, 2013.

THE FINAL PRAYER OF FATHER BENEDICT

In a December 1969 radio broadcast for Bavarian Rundfunk, forty-two-year-old Father Joseph Ratzinger spoke to his countrymen about the patriarch Abraham:

> He let go of what was safe, comprehensible, calculable, for the sake of what was unknown. And he did this in response to a single word from God. He had met God and placed all his future in God's hands; he dared to accept a new future that began in darkness.... Attachment to the accustomed world around him came to an end.... He no longer belongs to any fixed place and is therefore a stranger and a guest wherever he goes. [He] became homeless for the sake of a future, assured him by faith, and that he found a homeland precisely in the certainty of his faith.[222]

---

[222] Joseph Ratzinger, "Faith and Existence," in *Faith and the Future*, 40–42.

In this description of the trajectory of Abraham in Genesis, Joseph Ratzinger is presciently describing his own life in light of the decision he would make more than forty years later after speaking those words. In many ways, his abdication echoed across the centuries. It recalled Moses, who was not able to enter the Promised Land, a task entrusted to Joshua (cf. Deut. 34:4, 9). It also recalled the Ascension, when Jesus exhorted His disciples to complete the work that He had begun (cf. Luke 24:31).

Father Joseph Ratzinger was such a disciple.

In speaking about his decision to choose the name Benedict XVI, he referred to "the extraordinary figure of the great 'Patriarch of Western Monasticism', Saint Benedict, a powerful reminder of the indispensable Christian roots of his culture and civilization."[223] Saint Benedict of Nursia, who died in 543 at Monte Cassino,[224] spent time in solitude as a hermit in Subiaco—the very place where, fifteen hundred years later, Cardinal Ratzinger spoke of Europe's crisis with its faith and with itself. Now in our day, the very rebuilding of Europe that Benedict of Nursia achieved through his monastic legacy would have to be reconstructed again through courage, charity, and will.

Father Joseph Ratzinger was a disciple who could lead this reconstruction in our age.

"A humanism devoid of theology cannot stand," Theodor Haecker wrote in *Virgil: Father of the West*. Ratzinger believed

---

[223] Benedict XVI, "Reflection on the Name Chosen," April 27, 2005.

[224] The site of his first Benedictine monastery, whose influence extended beyond the life of its visionary. Its destruction during World War II is a symbol of the destruction wrought by that war, and its rebuilding is a testament to the triumphant ideology over that which was vanquished.

this to his core, and as the Roman pagan later became the great Dante character of Christianity's crowning poetry, the believer from Bavaria became the guide for an unbelieving world. He was unafraid to speak the truth, whether as a young professor amid the height of social upheaval or when proposing the root of mankind's nature to the most powerful world figures. Before Britain's elite at Westminster Hall, in a bold allusion to Church history, Benedict XVI evoked Saint Thomas More, whose opposition to King Henry VIII cost him his life. "He followed his conscience, even at the cost of displeasing the sovereign whose 'good servant' he was, because he chose to serve God first."[225] Benedict XVI, a modern man for all seasons, spoke in the same hall where Thomas More stood trial 470 years earlier showing us that loving Christ above all else prompts a fearlessness toward worldly affairs many desire but rarely achieve.

Joseph Ratzinger desired that in his remaining years he be called simply "Father Benedict."[226] It had been six hundred years since the last Roman Catholic Church papal abdication, and yet the seamlessness masked the radical transition, and the result something like a resurrection: a new vitality, a dawn of a new day.

At the conclusion of the Ash Wednesday liturgy on February 13, 2013, the liturgy that marked the final public Mass offered by Joseph Ratzinger, Secretary of State Bertone spoke before both the Pope and the packed congregation in Saint Peter's Basilica.

---

[225] Benedict XVI, address during a meeting with representatives of British society, including the diplomatic corps, politicians, academics and business leaders, September 17, 2010.

[226] Elise Harris, "The Request of a Retired Pope — Simply Call Me 'Father Benedict'," Catholic News Agency, December 9, 2014, accessed December 15, 2015, http://www.catholicnewsagency. com/.

"We would be less than honest, Your Holiness," Bertone began, "if we did not say that this evening there is a veil of sadness over our hearts." He continued, "In recent years, your teaching has … given light and warmth to our journey even, especially, at times when the clouds gather in the sky."

In the Vatican Television Center broadcast, while the Cardinal Secretary of State delivers his remarks, the camera cuts to various reaction shots: the row of bishops and cardinals, vested in purple and wearing their white miters, the congregation, and Pope Benedict himself, quietly listening, expressionless. "The Eucharist is a thanksgiving to God," Cardinal Bertone summarizes. "This evening, we want to give thanks to the Lord for the journey that the whole church has undertaken under the guidance of Your Holiness, and we want to say to you from the depths of our hearts, with great affection and admiration: thank you, for giving us the shining example of a 'simple and humble worker in the vineyard of the Lord'." Here, Benedict allows himself the slightest of smiles, recognizing the reference from April 19, 2005: "The cardinals have elected me," the then newly chosen Benedict XVI greeted the world, "a simple, humble worker in the vineyard of the Lord."

Eight years later, Cardinal Bertone ended his speech of gratitude by calling Pope Benedict a "laborer who knew at every moment to do what is most important: bring God to men and bring men to God." When Bertone finished, Benedict instantly rose to thank him. But as the Pope prepared for the Prayer after Communion, it was the congregation's turn. Just as spontaneous applause followed the homily before the conclave in 2005, a longer, extended, but bittersweet ovation trailed Bertone's speech this Wednesday in 2013. Keeping his eyes downcast, though gesturing at one point with his familiar two-handed wave, Benedict waited for the moment to subside. But still it persisted.

The Final Prayer of Father Benedict

During the ovation, sounding like heavy cascading ocean waves echoing throughout the basilica, the emotion of the moment, the realization that Benedict XVI was indeed stepping down, and the magnitude of his service and accomplishments all poured out. Off to the side, a prelate, sobbing, wiped tears from his eyes. Ever focused, Benedict bided his time by reading to himself, lips slightly moving, the final prayer. And after the congregation rose to their feet, continuing their applause, the bishops responded in sync by removing their miters.

The ovation sustained itself for nearly three minutes until Benedict finally interrupted it, gently but firmly in Italian: "Thank you.... Let us return to prayer. *Dominus Vobiscum* ..."[227]

---

[227] See "Cardinal Bertone Thanks Pope Benedict XVI — Ash Wednesday 2013," YouTube video, 6:31, posted by "Salt and Light," February 13, 2013, https://www.youtube.com/watch?v=6TJfIt63cbg.

JAMES F. DAY

James Day's writings on Pope Benedict XVI have appeared in *Catholic Exchange, Catholic World Report,* and *Crisis Magazine.* He has a BA in Latin from John Carroll University and an MFA from Loyola Marymount University. He lives with his wife in Orange County, California.

Sophia Institute

Sophia Institute is a nonprofit institution that seeks to nurture the spiritual, moral, and cultural life of souls and to spread the Gospel of Christ in conformity with the authentic teachings of the Roman Catholic Church.

Sophia Institute Press fulfills this mission by offering translations, reprints, and new publications that afford readers a rich source of the enduring wisdom of mankind.

Sophia Institute also operates two popular online Catholic resources: CrisisMagazine.com and CatholicExchange.com.

Crisis Magazine provides insightful cultural analysis that arms readers with the arguments necessary for navigating the ideological and theological minefields of the day. *Catholic Exchange* provides world news from a Catholic perspective as well as daily devotionals and articles that will help you to grow in holiness and live a life consistent with the teachings of the Church.

In 2013, Sophia Institute launched Sophia Institute for Teachers to renew and rebuild Catholic culture through service to Catholic education. With the goal of nurturing the spiritual, moral, and cultural life of souls, and an abiding respect for the role and work of teachers, we strive to provide materials and programs that are at once enlightening to the mind and ennobling to the heart; faithful and complete, as well as useful and practical.

Sophia Institute gratefully recognizes the Solidarity Association for preserving and encouraging the growth of our apostolate over the course of many years. Without their generous and timely support, this book would not be in your hands.

www.SophiaInstitute.com
www.CatholicExchange.com
www.CrisisMagazine.com
www.SophiaInstituteforTeachers.org

Sophia Institute Press® is a registered trademark of Sophia Institute.
Sophia Institute is a tax-exempt institution as defined by the
Internal Revenue Code, Section 501(c)(3). Tax I.D. 22-2548708.